KETO SLOW COOKER COOKBOOK

Make Your Body a Fat-Burning Machine with Delicious Meals Using the Slow Cooker | Get Ketogenic Weight Loss With Sugar-Free, Low-Cholesterol, Low-Carb Recipes & Meal Plan

By

Jimmy   Emmerich Pot

Table of Contents

CHAPTER 6. LUNCH

CHAPTER 7. DINNER

CHAPTER 8. POULTRY

CHAPTER 9. VEGETABLES

CHAPTER 11. SEAFOOD & FISH RECIPES

CHAPTER 12. SIDE DISH RECIPES

CHAPTER 13. DESSERT RECIPES

220. COCONUT CUPCAKES

221. ANISE HOT CHOCOLATE

222. CHOCOLATE MOUSSE

223. LIME MUFFINS

224. BLUEBERRY MUFFINS

225. LOW CARB BROWNIE

226. PECAN PIE

227. VANILLA FLAN

228. VANILLA PIE

229. CUSTARD

230. CRÈME BRULE

231. LAVA CAKE

232. KETO COCONUT HOT CHOCOLATE

233. AMBROSIA

234. DARK CHOCOLATE AND PEPPERMINT POTS

235. CREAMY VANILLA CUSTARD

236. COCONUT, CHOCOLATE, AND ALMOND TRUFFLE BAKE

237. PEANUT BUTTER, CHOCOLATE, AND PECAN CUPCAKES

238. VANILLA AND STRAWBERRY CHEESECAKE

239. COFFEE CREAMS WITH TOASTED SEED CRUMBLE TOPPING

240. LEMON CHEESECAKE

241. MACADAMIA FUDGE TRUFFLES

242. CHOCOLATE COVERED BACON CUPCAKES

243. SUGAR-FREE CHOCOLATE MOLTEN LAVA CAKE

244. BLUEBERRY LEMON CUSTARD CAKE

245. SLOW-COOKED PUMPKIN CUSTARD

246. ALMOND FLOUR MOCHA FUDGE CAKE

247. SLOW COOKER BREAD PUDDING

248. TIRAMISU BREAD PUDDING

249. CROCK POT SUGAR-FREE DAIRY-FREE FUDGE

250. POPPY SEED-LEMON BREAD

CONCLUSION

Introduction

The ketogenic diet is trendy, and for an excellent reason. It truly teaches healthy eating without forcing anyone into at risk. The success rate of keto is relatively high. While there are no specific numbers to suggest the exact rate, it is only fair to state that those who have the will to change their lifestyle and are okay adjusting to new eating habits, will make it through as a success story.

Limiting your carbohydrate intake, this diet causes your system to use fat instead of carbohydrates for energy. However, it is not a high protein diet. It involves moderate protein, low carbohydrate intake, and high fat intake.

Regardless of your lifestyle, everyone benefits from the keto diet in the following ways:

Weight Loss

Far more important than the visual aspect of excess weight is its negative influence on your body. Too much weight affects the efficiency of your body's blood flow, which in turn also affects how much oxygen your heart is able to pump to every part of your system. Too much weight also means that there are layers of fat covering your internal organs, which prevents them from working efficiently. It makes it hard to walk because it puts great pressure on your joints, and makes it very difficult to complete even regular daily tasks. A healthy weight allows your body to move freely and your entire internal system to work at its optimal levels.

Cognitive Focus

In order for your brain to function at its best, it needs to have balanced levels of all nutrients and molecules, because a balance allows it to focus on other things, such as working, studying, or creativity. If you eat carbs, the sudden insulin spike that comes with them will force your brain to stop whatever it was doing and to turn its focus on the correct breakdown of glucose molecules. This is why people often feel sleepy and with a foggy mind after high-carb meals. The keto diet keeps the balance strong, so that your brain does not have to deal with any sudden surprises.

Blood Sugar Control

If you already have diabetes, or are prone to it, then controlling your blood sugar is obviously of the utmost importance. However, even if you are not battling a type of diabetes at the moment, that doesn't mean that you are not in danger of developing it in the future. Most people forget that insulin is a finite resource in your body. You are given a certain amount of it, and it is gradually used up throughout your life. The more often you eat carbs, the more often your body needs to use insulin to break down the glucose; and when it reaches critically low levels of this finite resource, diabetes is formed.

Lower Cholesterol and Blood Pressure

Cholesterol and triglyceride levels maintain, or ruin, your arterial health. If your arteries are clogged up with cholesterol, they cannot efficiently transfer blood through your system, which in some cases even results in heart attacks. The keto diet keeps all of these levels at an optimal level, so that they do not interfere with your body's normal functioning.

Slow Cookers

Slow cookers are not new appliances in the culinary world. They have been around for decades; you might even have fond memories from your childhood of your parents serving your favorite dinner out of one. Slow cookers are very versatile because the cooking environment works the same no matter the cuisine. Knowing what slow cookers can and can't do is important for planning your meals, especially for a diet like keto.

In this chapter, you will learn slow-cooker basics such as which kind is best for your needs, how to ensure your recipes turn out great, and how to convert your traditional family favorites to work for you. Taking the mystery out of the slow cooker should give you the confidence to create spectacular keto meals as often as you want in order to reach your goals while eating well.

Some of the reasons to use a slow cooker include:

Enhances flavor: Cooking ingredients over several hours with spices, herbs, and other seasonings creates vegetables and proteins that burst with delicious flavors. This slow process allows the flavors to mellow and deepen for an enhanced eating experience.

Saves time: Cooking at home takes a great deal of time: prepping, sautéing, stirring, turning the heat up and down, and watching the meal so that it does not over- or undercook. If you're unable to invest the time, you might find yourself reaching for convenience foods instead of healthy choices. Slow cookers allow you to do other activities while the meal cooks. You can put your ingredients in the slow cooker in the morning and come home to a perfectly cooked meal.

Convenient: Besides the time-saving aspect, using a slow cooker can free up the stove and oven for other dishes. This can be very convenient for large holiday meals or when you want to serve a side dish and entrée as well as a delectable dessert. Clean up is simple when you use the slow cooker for messy meals because most inserts are nonstick or are easily cleaned with a little soapy water, and each meal is prepared in either just the machine or using one additional vessel to sauté ingredients. There is no wide assortment of pots, pans, and baking dishes to contend with at the end of the day.

Low heat production: If you have ever cooked dinner on a scorching summer afternoon, you will appreciate the low amount of heat produced by a slow cooker. Even after eight hours of operation, slow cookers do not heat up your kitchen and you will not be sweating over the hot stovetop. Slow cookers use about a third of the energy of conventional cooking methods, just a little more energy than a traditional light bulb.

Supports healthy eating: Cooking your food at high heat can reduce the nutrition profile of your foods, breaking down and removing the majority of vitamins, minerals, and antioxidants while producing unhealthy chemical compounds that can contribute to disease. Low-heat cooking retains all the goodness that you want for your diet.

Saves Money: Slow cookers save you money because of the low amount of electricity they use and because the best ingredients for slow cooking are the less expensive cuts of beef and heartier inexpensive vegetables. Tougher cuts of meat— brisket, chuck, shanks—break down beautifully to fork-tender goodness. Another cost-saving benefit is that most 6-quart slow cookers will produce enough of a recipe to stretch your meals over at least two days. Leftovers are one of the best methods for saving money.

Chapter 1.   Everything About the Ketogenic Diet

There are many low-carb diets available. One of the most popular is the "ketogenic diet". More and more people are turning to the ketogenic diet because of the various advantages this diet carries. The ketogenic diet is a powerful way to lose weight and offers multiple benefits leading to a healthy lifestyle that fad diets do not. In this chapter, you will learn everything you need to know about the ketogenic diet.

What is the Ketogenic Diet?

The ketogenic diet is a high-fat, moderate protein, low-carbohydrate diet. This diet concentrates on decreasing your carbohydrate intake and replacing it with healthy fats and proteins. Normally, your body burns carbohydrates to convert into glucose, which is then carried around your body and is essential for brain fuel.

The ketogenic diet was created to reach a state of ketosis. Ketosis is a metabolic state where your body produces ketones. Ketones are produced by your liver and used as fuel toward your body and brain instead of glucose. To make ketones, you must consume a substantial number of carbs and a bare minimum amount of proteins. The traditional ketogenic diet contains a 4:1 ratio by weight of fat to combined protein and carbohydrate. This is achieved by eliminating high-carbohydrate foods, such as starchy fruits, vegetables, breads, cereals, pasta and sugar, while increasing your intake of high-fat foods, such as nuts, cream and butter. The bottom line is the ketogenic diet is a low-carb diet useful in burning body fat.

Lose Weight Faster with the Ketogenic Diet than Other Diets

Obesity has become one of the largest health epidemics in the world. Many have tried multiple methods to fight obesity and excess weight, but their methods were not successful. To overcome obesity and lose weight, you must change your diet. The ketogenic diet has worked for many to preserve muscle mass and shed excess fat, without putting much effort.

The sole purpose of the ketogenic diet is to make your body enter a state of glycogen deprivation and maintain a state of ketosis, which is great for weight loss. Usually, in carb-based diets, carbohydrates are transformed into glucose, which is then used as the main fuel source for the body and brain. The remaining glucose converts to glycogen and gets stored in your liver for later use. When your glycogen levels are full, the excess is stored as fat, thus leading to weight gain.

This means that the main cause of weight gain is not eating fats, but the excessive consumption of carbs. Once you eliminate or reduce your carb intake and raise your fat intake, your body changes from burning carbs for energy to burning fats for energy. This means that the excess fats stored in your body will be burned for your energy source, consequently leading to weight loss.

Alongside, the ketogenic lifestyle also helps suppressing your appetite. This is largely because the foods you eat under the ketogenic diet, like fats and protein are quite filling; thus, you will stay full longer and don't feel the urge to eat often.

Chapter 2.   Slow Cooker Bases

Slow cooking is familiar to most people. In fact, it's one of the oldest forms of cooking, because meat and veggies had to be stewed for a long time to make them soft (and safe) enough to eat. However, there was no specific cooking device designed for slow cooking until Irving Naxon. He patented the Naxon Beanery in 1940. In 1970, Rival bought the company, and re-released the electric pot with a new name: The Crock-Pot.

It came at the perfect time in human history. Women were becoming busier, and didn't have time to babysit a stove. The Crock-Pot let them start a meal at the beginning of the day, go to work, and then come back to finish it. They could also let a meal cook overnight. The concept of a slow cooker took off, and soon, there were 40 companies producing different versions of them.

After a brief stall in sales in the 1980's (the microwave came out), the slow cooker is still going strong. Improved features like tighter lids, cooking programs, and dishwasher-safe interiors have helped keep the slow cooker a staple in most homes.

Using a slow cooker

Slow cookers are easy to use, and are essentially the same no matter what brand you have. There's just three parts: the actual slow cooker itself which houses the electric parts; the interior pot, which is removable; and the lid. On the slow cooker, there will be a control knob or control panel, which will be slightly different depending on the brand and how "fancy" your cooker is. The most basic ones will have a "high" and "low" heat setting. Others may have a "medium" heat setting, "keep warm," and timers, so you can program the cooker to start and end at a certain time without you present. Generally, slow cookers have a temperature between 174 and199 degree F.

When you're ready to prepare a meal in your slow cooker, always read the recipe. You might be told to cook ingredients like garlic or onion in a skillet first before adding to your slow cooker. Sometimes you add ingredients in stages, because some take a shorter time. While most recipes have liquid, there are some that don't, either because the ingredients generate their own moisture, or it's just not a recipe that needs it.

When the meal is ready, make sure whatever meat you've used (if you've used any) is cooked to a safe temperature. After you've enjoyed your meal and it's time to clean up, you can wash out the interior pot and inside of the lid with a soft sponge, soap, and water. To clean the outside of the cooker, just wipe down with a damp paper towel. Easy!

What do you do when something goes wrong?

As easy as using a slow cooker is, sometimes there are problems. Luckily, there are simple solutions. Here's what to do:

Food is burned

The low temperature of a slow cooker usually ensures no burning happens, but sometimes food is just really sensitive. This problem is easily solved by lining the inside of your cooker pot with foil or inserts made specifically for slow cookers. This also makes clean-up way easier, so some people just use them all the time.

The meal has too much liquid

This usually happens when you cook a recipe usually done in the oven or on the stovetop, and forget to reduce the liquid. Slow cookers lose very little liquid during the cooking process, so reduce the original amount by 50%. If you're cooking something like a whole chicken, you don't even need to put extra liquid in, because the chicken renders its own fat. If you are nervous about cooking anything "dry," just a tablespoon of liquid is sufficient. To get rid of excess liquid from a finished meal, turn the cooker back on to the highest setting it has, and leave the lid off. After an hour, the liquid should have evaporated.

The cooker is smoking when you turn it on

This is a scary sight. What it means is there's food or oil in the cooker itself, by the heating element. If this is the first time you've used the cooker, it's most likely oil from the manufacturing process, and it should burn off quickly. If it's an old cooker, turn off the cooker and let it cool. Take out the pot and clean up around the inside.

The food is cooked unevenly

When you put a bunch of ingredients together and cook them for a long time, some will be done perfectly and some may be mushy. The best course of action is always to cut things into the same size, and add the quicker-cooking ingredients (like vegetables and seafood) later. You'll see this in many of the recipes.

Choosing a slow cooker

Because there are so many slow cookers out there, which ones are the best? You want to consider size, construction, functions, and price. The smallest cookers are only 3.5 quarts, while bigger ones can go up to 7 quarts. You probably want a larger slow cooker, because a common reason for buying one is to prepare food that can be used for leftovers. You also want one that can fit additional inserts, like ramekins, when you're cooking individual desserts.

As for construction, whenever there's food involved, you want to avoid materials like aluminum. Look for lead-free and ceramic-free. Stainless-steel is always best. A glass lid is also preferable, because it's easily cleaned and you can see what's happening in the cooker without opening it, and letting out heat.

Slow cookers have gotten a lot more technologically-advanced over the years, so the sky's the limit. One Crock-Pot model even has an app where you can control the temperature and time of your cooker, without even being in the house. Others are very basic, with just the knob for "high" or "low" heat.

This is where price tends to come in - the more cool features, the more you'll pay. That remote-app Crock-Pot is over $100. You should also expect to pay more for a slow cooker that is built to last. The best ones keep on cooking for decades. Think of it as an investment. You're more likely to cook at home more with a slow cooker, so if you usually eat out a lot, you'll save a lot of money. It's your choice, though, so consider all the factors and your budget to make the best decision for your family.

One of the more current explanations people give for getting a slow cooker is that they're trying out a new eating lifestyle. One of those is the ketogenic diet. What is it? How does it work?

Chapter 3.   How to Use the Slow Cooker, Tips and Tricks

Slow cookers have changed a lot over the years. These days you can purchase models that range from very simple models all the way to ones that look like they should be on a space station. When buying the right model for your needs, you have to consider what you are cooking, how many portions, and if you will be home during the cooking process. All these factors are important when deciding on the size, shape, and features of your slow cooker.

Size and Shape

Slow cookers come in a multitude of sizes and shapes, so it is important to consider your needs and what will work best for the type of food prepared on the keto diet. There are models that range from ½-quart to large 8-quart models and everything in-between.

The small slow cookers (½-quart to 2-quart) are usually used for dips or sauces, as well as recipes designed for one person. Medium-sized slow cookers (3-quart to 4-quart) are great for baking or for meals that create food for two to three people. The slow cooker recommended for most of the recipes in this book is the 5-quart to 6-quart model because it is perfect for the large cuts of meat on the keto diet and can prepare food for four people, including leftovers. The enormous 7-quart to 8-quart appliance is meant for very large meals. If you have money in your budget, owning both a 3-quart and 6-quart model would be the best of both worlds.

When it comes to shapes, you will have to decide between round, oval, and rectangular. Round slow cookers are fine for stews and chili but do not work well for large pieces of meat. These should probably not be your choice. Oval and rectangular slow cookers both allow for the ingredients you will use regularly that are large, like roasts, ribs, and chops, and have the added advantage of fitting loaf pans, ramekins, and casserole dishes, as well. Some desserts and breads are best cooked in another container placed in the slow cooker, and you will see several recipes in this book that use that technique.

Features

Now that you know the size and shape of the recommended slow cooker, it is time to consider what you want this appliance to do for you. Depending on your budget, at a minimum you want a slow cooker with temperature controls that cover warm, low, and high, as well as a removable insert. These are the primary features of the bare-bones models that will get the job done. However, if you want to truly experience a set-it-and-forget-it appliance that creates the best meals possible in this cooking environment, you might want to consider the following features:

Digital programmable controls: You can program temperature, when the slow cooker starts, how long it cooks, and when the slow cooker switches to warm.

Glass lid: These are heavier and allow you to look into the slow cooker without removing them, so there is little heat loss. Opt for a lid with clamps, and you can transport your cooked meal easily to parties and gatherings if needed.

Temperature probe: Once you have a slow cooker with this feature, you will wonder how you cooked previously without it. The temperature probe allows you to cook your meat, poultry, and egg dishes to an exact temperature and then switches to warm when completed.

Precooking feature: Some models have a precooking feature that allows you to brown your meat and poultry right in the insert. You will still have to take the time to do this step, but you won't have a skillet to clean afterward.

TIPS FOR SLOW-COOKING SUCCESS

Slow cookers are simple to use, but you can increase your success with a few tips and techniques. In the following list, some tips are suggestions, and some should be considered more seriously for safety or health reasons. The intent is to provide the best information possible so that your meals are delicious and easy.

Always

Read the user manual and any other literature. You will find an assortment of instructions included in the slow-cooker box, so take the time to sit down and read everything completely before using a new device. You might think you know how everything works, but each model is a little different, and it is best to be informed about all of the things your slow cooker can do.

Grease the insert of the slow cooker before cooking. Cleaning a slow cooker insert can be a challenge, so grease the insert, even for soups and stews. You don't want to scrub the insert with abrasive brushes or scraping bits of cooked-on food off, because you will wreck its nonstick surface.

Add dairy and herbs at the end of the cooking process. As stated elsewhere in this book, dairy and fresh herbs do not hold up well during long cooking times. Dairy splits and creates a grainy, unpleasant texture, and herbs lose their flavor, color, and texture. Always add these ingredients at the end.

Always cut your ingredients into similar-sized pieces. Slow cookers are not meant to be used for staggered cooking recipes such as stir-fries, where the more delicate ingredients are added last to avoid overcooking. Evenly sized pieces mean your ingredients will be ready at the same time, and your meals will be cooked evenly.

Adjust your seasonings. Slow cookers can have an unexpected effect on herbs and spices so it is important to taste and adjust at the end of the process. Some spices, such as curry or cayenne, can get more intense, while the long cooking time can reduce the impact of dried herbs. It is best to hold off on too much salt until the very end as well, because it will get stronger.

Never

Use frozen meats or poultry. The ingredients in slow cookers need to reach 140°F within 4 hours for food safety, so large cuts of meat or poultry should be fully thawed. You can add small frozen items like meatballs to a slow cooker because these can come to temperature within this time range.

Place your insert right from the refrigerator into the slow cooker. When you remove your previously prepared meal from the refrigerator, let the insert sit out at room temperature for 30 minutes or so to avoid cracking it with extreme temperature changes. Also, never remove the hot insert from your slow cooker and place it on a cold surface.

Resume cooking after a power outage of over two hours. Power outages can happen in any season, and for food-safety reasons, you have to err on the side of caution. If an outage lasts for more than two hours, especially during the first few hours of the cooking time, you need to discard the food because the amount of time spent in the food danger zone (40°F to 140°F) will have been too long. If the outage is less than two hours and it occurs after your food has been cooking for at least four hours, then you can resume cooking until the end of the original time or transfer the food to a pot or casserole dish and finish it on the stove or in the oven. When in doubt, throw the food out.

Use the recommended cooking times in high altitudes. As with most other cooking methods, slow cookers need more cooking time if you live above an altitude of 3,000 feet. The liquid in the slow cooker will simmer at a lower temperature, so high-heat settings are recommended, or if you can program the slow cooker, then set it to maintain the food at 200°F or higher. You can also use a temperature probe set to 165°F internal temperature if your slow cooker has this feature.

Chapter 4.   The Ketogenic Kitchen

Your kitchen will now become ketogenic, so that means stocking up on all the great foods that will usher your body into ketosis. Your kitchen will also have a slow cooker, which is your new best friend on this new eating journey. This chapter will present a list of what to buy, and how the slow cooker fits into being keto.

What To Stock

When you go grocery-shopping, you always want your cart full of proteins, vegetables, good fats, baking supplies (if you're out), full-fat dairy, and some fruit, nuts, and seeds. Here's a list of what should always be in your kitchen:

Proteins

- Ground grass-fed beef
- Organic chicken
- Ground turkey
- Frozen fish fillets
- Canned tuna
- Bone broth

Oils

- Olive oil (cold-pressed)
- High-quality coconut oil

Dairy

- Grass-fed butter
- Heavy cream
- Plain, whole-milk Greek yogurt
- A hard cheese (in block form)
- A soft cheese

Non-dairy

- Unsweetened almond milk (or your favorite nut milk)
- Full-fat coconut milk
- Coconut cream

Fruit

- Blueberries (fresh or frozen)
- Raspberries (fresh or frozen)
- Strawberries (fresh or frozen)
- Avocados

Vegetables

(If you don't like a certain vegetable, just get more of your favorites)

- Dark leafy greens (Swiss chard, kale, and/or spinach)
- Cauliflower
- Celery
- Zucchini
- Cucumbers
- Bell peppers
- Tomatoes
- Garlic
- Onions

Nuts + seeds

- Whole almonds (unsalted)
- Pecans
- Macadamia nuts or Brazil nuts
- Chia seeds

- Unsweetened almond nut butter

Flours

- Coconut flour
- Almond flour
- Flax Meal

Baking supplies

- Aluminum-free baking powder
- Unsweetened dark cocoa powder
- Rodelle pure vanilla extract
- Sukrin Gold (brown sugar substitute)
- Stevia + erythritol (or blend of both)
- Dark baking chocolate
- Cacao nibs or sugar-free chocolate chips
- Unsweetened shredded coconut

Cooking supplies

- Dry herbs
- Spices
- Homemade ketchup
- Homemade yellow mustard

How The Slow Cooker Helps You Succeed On The Ketogenic Diet

The slow cooker is defined by its convenience, which is very important when you're changing your diet. There are three other reasons why the slow cooker can help you transition successfully into ketosis, and stay there:

It breaks down even tough meat

The ketogenic diet has you eating a lot of meat, which is one of the best ingredients to make in a slow cooker. Even cheap, tough cuts of meat become tender and juicy in a slow cooker, so every meal is tasty.

It makes a lot of food

Leftovers will become very important on the ketogenic diet, because you don't want to have to make separate meals all the time. The slow cooker was designed to cook a lot of food at once, so you can make big recipes or double batches for dinner and tomorrow's lunch.

It's versatile

As you'll see in the recipes, the slow cooker can make just about everything. That simplifies the whole "healthy cooking" process, and just makes life way easier. You're a busy person with deadlines and commitments, and you don't want to have to use a bunch of different devices to cook different meals. With the slow cooker, you can make everything from eggs to cakes.

Chapter 5.   Breakfast

1. Cherry Tomatoes Thyme Asparagus Frittata

Preparation time: 15 minutes

Cooking time: 6 hours

Servings: 6

Ingredients:

- 2 tablespoons unsalted butter, ghee, or extra-virgin olive oil
- 12 large eggs
- ¼ cup heavy (whipping) cream
- 1 tablespoon minced fresh thyme
- ½ teaspoon kosher salt
- ¼ teaspoon freshly ground black pepper
- 1½ cups shredded sharp white Cheddar cheese, divided
- ½ cup grated Parmesan cheese
- 16 cherry tomatoes

- 16 asparagus spears

Directions:

1. Glaze the inside of the slow cooker with the butter.
2. In the slow cooker, beat the eggs, then whisk in the heavy cream, thyme, salt, and pepper.
3. Add ¾ cup of Cheddar cheese and the Parmesan cheese and stir to mix.
4. Sprinkle the remaining ¾ cup of Cheddar cheese over the top.
5. Scatter the cherry tomatoes over the frittata.
6. Arrange the asparagus spears decoratively over the top. Cook
7. within 6 hours on low or 3 hours on soaring. Serve.

Nutrition:

Calories: 370

Fat: 29g

Carbs: 4g

Protein: 24g

2. Healthy Low Carb Walnut Zucchini Bread

Preparation time: 15 minutes

Cooking time: 3 hours & 10 minutes

Servings: 12

Ingredients:

- 3 eggs
- 1/2 cup walnuts, chopped
- 2 cups zucchini, shredded
- 2 tsp vanilla
- 1/2 cup pure all-purpose sweetener
- 1/3 cup coconut oil, softened
- 1/2 tsp baking soda
- 1 1/2 Tsp baking powder
- 2 tsp cinnamon
- 1/3 cup coconut flour
- 1 cup almond flour
- 1/2 Tsp salt

Directions:

1. Mix the almond flour, baking powder, cinnamon, baking soda, coconut flour, and salt in a bowl. Set aside.
2. Whisk eggs, vanilla, sweetener, and oil in another bowl.
3. Put dry batter to the wet and fold well. Add walnut and zucchini and fold well.
4. Pour batter into the silicone bread pan. Place the bread pan into the slow cooker on the rack.
5. Cook on high within 3 hours. Cut the bread loaf into the slices and serve.

Nutrition:

Calories: 174

Fat: 15.4 g

Carb: 5.8 g

Protein: 5.3 g

3. Savory Creamy Breakfast Casserole

Preparation time: 15 minutes

Cooking time: 6 hours

Servings: 8

Ingredients:

- 1 tablespoon unsalted butter, Ghee
- 10 large eggs, beaten
- 1 cup heavy (whipping) cream
- 1½ cups shredded sharp Cheddar cheese, divided
- ½ cup grated Romano cheese
- ½ teaspoon kosher salt
- ¼ teaspoon freshly ground black pepper
- 8 ounces thick-cut ham, diced
- ¾ head broccoli, cut into small florets
- ½ onion, diced

Directions:

1. Grease the slow cooker with the butter.
2. Whisk the eggs, heavy cream, ½ cup of Cheddar cheese, the Romano cheese, salt, and pepper inside the slow cooker.
3. Stir in the ham, broccoli, and onion. Put the remaining 1 cup of Cheddar cheese over the top.
4. Cook within 6 hours on low or 3 hours on high. Serve hot.

Nutrition:

Calories: 465

Fat: 36g

Carbs: 7g

Protein: 28g

4. Low-Carb Hash Brown Breakfast Casserole

Preparation time: 15 minutes

Cooking time: 6 hours

Servings: 6

Ingredients:

- 1 tablespoon unsalted butter, Ghee
- 12 large eggs
- ½ cup heavy cream
- 1 teaspoon kosher salt
- ½ teaspoon ground black pepper
- ½ teaspoon ground mustard
- 1 head cauliflower, shredded or minced
- 1 onion, diced
- 10 ounces cooked sausage links, sliced
- 2 cups shredded Cheddar cheese, divided

Directions:

1. Grease the slow cooker with the butter.

2. Beat the eggs, then whisk in heavy cream, 1 teaspoon of salt, ½ teaspoon of pepper, and the ground mustard in a large bowl.

3. Spread about one-third of the cauliflower in an even layer in the bottom of the cooker.

4. Layer one-third of the onions over the cauliflower, then one-third of the sausage, and top with ½ cup of Cheddar cheese. Season with salt and pepper. Repeat twice.

5. Pour the egg batter evenly over the layered Ingredients, then sprinkle the remaining ½ cup Cheddar cheese on top—Cook within 6 hours on low. Serve hot.

Nutrition:

Calories: 523

Fat: 40g

Carbs: 7g

Protein: 33g

5. Onion Broccoli Cream Cheese Quiche

Preparation time: 15 minutes

Cooking time: 2 hours & 25 minutes

Servings: 8

Ingredients:

- 9 eggs
- 2 cups cheese, shredded and divided
- 8 oz. cream cheese
- 1/4 Tsp onion powder
- 3 cups broccoli, cut into florets
- 1/4 Tsp pepper
- 3/4 Tsp salt

Directions:

1. Add broccoli into the boiling water and cook for 3 minutes. Drain well and set aside to cool.
2. Add eggs, cream cheese, onion powder, pepper, and salt in mixing bowl and beat until well combined.
3. Spray slow cooker from inside using cooking spray.
4. Add cooked broccoli into the slow cooker then sprinkle half cup cheese.
5. Pour egg mixture over broccoli and cheese mixture.
6. Cook on high within 2 hours and 15 minutes.
7. Once it is done, then sprinkle the remaining cheese and cover for 10 minutes or until cheese melted. Serve.

Nutrition:

Calories 296

Fat 24.3 g

Carb 3.9 g

Protein 16.4 g

6. Delicious Thyme Sausage Squash

Preparation time: 15 minutes

Cooking time: 6 hours

Servings: 4

Ingredients:

- 2 tablespoons extra-virgin olive oil
- 14 ounces smoked chicken sausage, thinly sliced
- ¼ cup chicken broth
- 1 onion, halved and sliced

- ½ medium butternut squash, peeled, diced
- 1 small green bell pepper, strips
- ½ small red bell pepper, strips
- ½ small yellow bell pepper, strips
- 2 teaspoons snipped fresh thyme or ½ teaspoon dried thyme, crushed
- ½ teaspoon kosher salt
- ½ teaspoon freshly ground black pepper
- 1 cup shredded Swiss cheese

Directions:

1. Combine the olive oil, sausage, broth, onion, butternut squash, bell peppers, thyme, salt, and pepper in the slow cooker. Toss to mix. Cook within 6 hours on low.
2. Before serving, sprinkle the Swiss cheese over the top, cover, and cook for about 3 minutes more to melt the cheese.

Nutrition:

Calories: 502

Fat: 38g

Carbs: 12g

Protein: 27g

7. Mexican Style Breakfast Casserole

Preparation time: 15 minutes

Cooking time: 5 hours

Servings: 5

Ingredients:

- 5 eggs

- 6 ounces pork sausage, cooked, drained
- ½ cup 1% milk
- ½ teaspoon garlic powder
- 2 jalapeños, deseeded, finely chopped
- ½ teaspoon ground cumin
- ½ teaspoon ground coriander
- 1 ½ cups chunky salsa
- 1 ½ cup pepper Jack cheese, shredded
- Salt to taste
- Pepper to taste
- ¼ cup fresh cilantro

Directions:

1. Coat the slow cooker with cooking spray. Mix the eggs, salt, pepper, plus milk in a bowl.
2. Add garlic powder, cumin, coriander, and sausage and mix well.
3. Pour the mixture into the slow cooker. Set the slow cooker on 'Low' within 4-5 hours or on 'High' for 2-3 hours. Place toppings of your choice and serve.

Nutrition:

Calories: 320

Fat: 24.1 g

Carb: 5.2 g

Protein: 17.9 g

8. Almond Lemon Blueberry Muffins

Preparation time: 15 minutes

Cooking time: 3 hours

Servings: 3

Ingredients:

- 1 cup almond flour
- 1 large egg
- 3 drops stevia
- ¼ cup fresh blueberries
- ¼ teaspoon lemon zest, grated
- ¼ teaspoon pure lemon extract
- ½ cup heavy whipping cream
- 2 tablespoons butter, melted
- ½ teaspoon baking powder

Directions:

1. Whisk the egg into a bowl. Add the rest of the fixing, and mix.
2. Pour batter into lined or greased muffin molds. Pour up to ¾ of the cup.
3. Pour 6 ounces of water into the slow cooker. Place an aluminum foil at the bottom, and the muffin molds inside.
4. Set the slow cooker on 'High' within 2-3 hours. Let it cool in the cooker for a while.
5. Remove from the cooker. Loosen the edges of the muffins. Invert on to a plate and serve.

Nutrition:

Calories: 223

Fat: 21g

Carb: 5g

Protein: 6 g

9. Healthy Veggie Omelet

Preparation time: 15 minutes

Cooking time: 1 hour & 40 minutes

Servings: 4

Ingredients:

- 6 eggs
- 1 tsp parsley, dried
- 1 tsp garlic powder
- 1 bell pepper, diced
- 1/2 cup onion, sliced
- 1 cup spinach
- 1/2 cup almond milk, unsweetened
- 4 egg whites
- Pepper
- Salt

Directions:

1. Grease the slow cooker from inside using cooking spray.
2. Whisk egg whites, eggs, parsley, garlic powder, almond milk, pepper, and salt in a large bowl.
3. Stir in bell peppers, spinach, and onion. Pour egg batter into the slow cooker.
4. Cook on high within 90 minutes or until egg sets. Cut into the slices and serve.

Nutrition:

Calories: 200

Fat: 13.9 g

Carb: 5.8 g

Protein 13.4 g

10.   Arugula Cheese Herb Frittata

Preparation time: 15 minutes

Cooking time: 3 hours & 10 minutes

Servings: 6

Ingredients:

- 8 eggs
- 3/4 cup goat cheese, crumbled
- 1/2 cup onion, sliced
- 1 1/2 cups red peppers, roasted and chopped
- 4 cups baby arugula
- 1 tsp oregano, dried
- 1/3 cup almond milk
- Pepper
- Salt

Directions:

1. Grease the slow cooker using a cooking spray. Whisk eggs, oregano, and almond milk in a mixing bowl.
2. Put pepper and salt. Arrange red peppers, onion, arugula, and cheese into the slow cooker.
3. Pour egg batter into the slow cooker over the vegetables. Cook on low within 3 hours. Serve hot and enjoy.

Nutrition:

Calories: 178

Fat: 12.8 g

Carb: 6 g

Protein: 11.4 g

11.   Yummy Cauliflower Crust Breakfast Pizza

Preparation time: 15 minutes

Cooking time: 5 hours

Servings: 4

Ingredients:

- 2 large eggs
- 3 cups riced cauliflower
- 1 cup grated Parmesan cheese
- 8 ounces goat cheese, divided
- ½ teaspoon kosher salt
- 1 tablespoon extra-virgin olive oil
- Grated zest of 1 lemon

Directions:

1. Beat the eggs, cauliflower, Parmesan cheese, 2 ounces of goat cheese, and the salt until well mixed in a large bowl.
2. Grease the slow cooker using the olive oil. Press the cauliflower batter in an even layer around the cooker's bottom and extend slightly up the sides.
3. Stir the remaining 6 ounces of goat cheese and the lemon zest in a small bowl. Dollop spoonsful onto the cauliflower crust, distributing it evenly.
4. Set the lid on the slow cooker, but prop it slightly open with a chopstick or wooden spoon. Cook within 6 hours on low or 3 hours on high, until the edges are slightly browned.
5. When finished, turn off the cooker but let the pizza sit in it 30 minutes before serving. Serve warm.

Nutrition:

Calories: 389

Fat: 29g

Carbs: 6g

Protein: 24g

12.   Parmesan Zucchini Paprika & Ricotta Frittata

Preparation time: 15 minutes

Cooking time: 6 hours

Servings: 6

Ingredients:

- 2 medium zucchinis, shredded
- 1 teaspoon kosher salt, divided
- 1 tablespoon extra-virgin olive oil
- 12 large eggs
- 3 tablespoons heavy (whipping) cream
- 3 tablespoons finely chopped fresh parsley
- 1 tablespoon fresh thyme
- ½ teaspoon paprika
- ½ teaspoon freshly ground black pepper
- 6 ounces ricotta cheese
- 12 cherry tomatoes, halved
- ½ cup grated Parmesan cheese

Directions:

1. Toss the shredded zucchini with ½ teaspoon of salt in a colander set in the sink. Let the zucchini sit for a few minutes, then squeeze out the excess liquid with your hands.
2. Grease the slow cooker with olive oil.
3. Beat the eggs, heavy cream, parsley, thyme, paprika, pepper, and the remaining ½ teaspoon of salt in a large bowl.

4. Put the zucchini and stir. Transfer the mixture to the prepared insert.

5. Using a large spoon, dollop the ricotta cheese into the egg mixture, distributing it evenly.

6. Top with the tomatoes and sprinkle the Parmesan cheese over the top. Set to cook within 6 hours on low or 3 hours on high. Serve at room temperature.

Nutrition:

Calories: 291

Fat: 22g

Carbs: 4g

Protein: 18g

13.   Scrambled Eggs with Smoked Salmon

Preparation time: 15 minutes

Cooking time: 2 hours

Servings: 6

Ingredients:

- Smoked salmon ¼ lb.
- eggs12 pcs fresh
- heavy cream½ cup
- almond flour¼ cup
- Salt and black pepper at will
- Butter2 tablespoons
- fresh chives at will

Directions:

1. Cut the slices of salmon. Set aside for garnish. Chop the rest of the salmon into small pieces.
2. Take a medium bowl, whisk the eggs and cream together. Add half of the chopped chives, season eggs with salt and pepper. Add flour.
3. Dissolve the butter over medium heat, then pour into the mixture. Grease the Slow Cooker with oil or cooking spray.
4. Add salmon pieces to the mixture, pour it into the Slow Cooker. Set to cook on low within 2 hours.
5. Garnish the dish with remaining salmon, chives. Serve warm and enjoy!

Nutrition:

Calories: 263

Carbs: 0g

Fat: 0g

Protein: 0g

14.   Garlic-Parmesan Asparagus Crock Pot

Preparation time: 15 minutes

Cooking time: 1 hour

Servings: 6

Ingredients:

- olive oil extra virgin2 tablespoons
- minced garlic2 teaspoons
- egg 1 pcs fresh
- garlic salt1/2 teaspoon
- fresh asparagus12 ounces
- Parmesan cheese1/3 cup
- Pepper at will

Directions:

1. Peel the garlic and mince it. Wash the asparagus. Shred the Parmesan cheese.
2. Take a medium-sized bowl combine oil, garlic, cracked egg, and salt

together. Whisk everything well.

3. Cover the green beans and coat them well.

4. Spread the cooking spray over the Slow Cooker's bottom, put the coated asparagus, season with the shredded cheese. Toss.

5. Cook on high within 1 hour. Once the time is over, you may also season with the rest of the cheese. Serve.

Nutrition:

Calories: 88

Carbs: 7g

Fat: 9g

Protein: 7g

15.   Persian Omelet Crock Pot

Preparation time: 15 minutes

Cooking time: 3 hours

Servings: 14

Ingredients:

- olive oil 2 tablespoons
- butter 1 tablespoons
- red onion 1 large
- green onions 4 pcs
- garlic 2 cloves
- Spinach 2 oz.
- fresh chives ¼ cup
- cilantro leaves ¼ cup
- parsley leaves ¼ cup
- fresh dill 2 tablespoons
- Kosher salt and black pepper at will

- pine nuts ¼ cup
- eggs 9 large
- whole milk ¼ cup
- Greek yogurt 1 cup

Directions:

1. Take a saucepan to melt the butter. Add red onion, stirring occasionally; it takes about 8-9 minutes.
2. Add green onions, garlic, continue cooking for 4 minutes. Put the spinach, chives, parsley, and cilantro, add salt and pepper at will. Remove the skillet, add the pine nuts.
3. Take a bowl, crack the eggs, add milk, and a little pepper and whisk. Mix the eggs with veggie mixture.
4. Open the Slow Cooker and spread the cooking spray over the bottom and sides. Pour the mix into the Slow Cooker. Cook on low for 3 hours. Serve with Greek yogurt. Bon Appetite!

Nutrition:

Calories: 220

Carbs: 9g

Fat: 16g

Protein: 12g

16.   Broccoli and Cheese Stuffed Squash

Preparation time: 15 minutes

Cooking time: 3 hours

Servings: 7

Ingredients:

- squash 1 pcs, halves

- broccoli florets 2 cups
- garlic 3 pcs
- red pepper flakes 1 teaspoon
- Italian season 1 teaspoon
- mozzarella cheese 1/2 cup
- Parmesan cheese 1/3 cup
- cooking spray
- salt and pepper at will

Directions:

1. Grease the Slow Cooker. Put the squash halves in the Slow Cooker.
2. Add a little bit of water at room temperature to the bottom of the Slow Cooker.
3. Put on low within 2 hours, until squash is mild. Take off the squash and let it cool for about 15 minutes.
4. Take a medium skillet, add pepper flakes and a little bit oil and cook for 20 seconds, stir it continuously.
5. Add broccoli, minced garlic to the skillet, continue to stir thoroughly, until the broccoli is tender.
6. Take the squash and using a fork; take off the flesh of the squash. Add it to the medium bowl and conjoin with the broccoli mixture.
7. Shred the Parmesan cheese carefully, put salt and pepper at will, and add seasoning to the mixture. Mix well and fill the squash.
8. Put the filled squash again in the Slow Cooker, dress with mozzarella cheese each squash half.
9. Cover and cook on low within 1 hour. Remove the dish and serve.

Nutrition:

Calories: 230

Carbs: 22g

Fat: 6g

Protein: 21g

17. Garlic Butter Keto Spinach

Preparation time: 15 minutes

Cooking time: 1 hour

Servings: 4

Ingredients:

- salted butter 2 tablespoons
- garlic, minced 4 cloves
- Baby spinach 8 oz.
- Pinch of salt
- lemon juice 1 teaspoons

Directions:

1. Heat-up a little skillet, add the butter, and melt. Sautee the garlic until a bit tender.
2. Spray the cooking spray over the bottom of the Slow Cooker.
3. Put the spinach into the Slow Cooker, season with salt and lemon juice, tender garlic, butter.
4. Put to cook on low within 1 hour. Garnish with fresh lemon wedges. Serve hot.

Nutrition:

Calories: 38

Carbs: 2g

Fat: 3g

Protein: 2g

18. Keto Crock Pot Tasty Onions

Preparation time: 15 minutes

Cooking time: 6 hours

Servings: 4

Ingredients:

- Onions 4 (or 5) large pcs, sliced
- Butter or coconut oil 4 tablespoon
- Coconut aminos 1/4 cup
- Splenda (optional)
- Salt and pepper

Directions:

1. Place the onion slices into the Slow Cooker. Top the onion slices with coconut amino and butter; you might add Splenda at will.
2. Cook it on low during 6-7 hours. Serve over the grilled vegetables.

Nutrition:

Calories: 38

Carbs: 9g

Fat: 0g

Protein: 0g

19. Crock Pot Benedict Casserole

Preparation time: 15 minutes

Cooking time: 4 hours

Servings: 7

Ingredients:

- For the Casserole
- English muffin 1 large, cut into portions
- Canadian bacon1 lb. thick-cut
- eggs 10 large
- milk 1 cup
- salt and pepper
- for garnish
- For the Sauce
- egg 6 yolks
- lemon juice 1 1/2 tablespoon
- unsalted butter, melted1 1/2 sticks
- salt
- pinch of cayenne

Directions:

1. For the muffin: Using a medium-sized skillet, melt the butter. Add coconut and almond flour, egg, salt, and stir everything well. Add baking soda. Grease the Slow Cooker with cooking spray. Pour the mixture, put on low for 2 hours. Remove once done.
2. Grease again the Slow Cooker with cooking spray, cut the muffin into equal pieces, put on the bottom.
3. Slice the bacon, sprinkle half of it over top of the muffin pieces.
4. Whisk milk, eggs, season with salt and black pepper in a large bowl.
5. Pour the egg batter evenly over the muffin pieces and top with the rest of the bacon.
6. Cook on low within 2 hours in the slow cooker. Remove, and keep the muffins covered before serving.
7. To make the sauce, set up a double boiler, put the egg yolks, squeeze lemon juice in a bowl, and mix.

8. Put your bowl over the double boiler, continue whisking carefully; the bowl mustn't get too hot.

9. Put in the melted butter while continuing to whisk.

10.   Season with salt and pepper. You may also add a little bit more lemon juice or cayenne.

11.   Serve and enjoy.

Nutrition:

Calories: 286

Carbs: 16g

Fat: 19g

Protein: 14g

20.   Crustless Crock Pot Spinach Quiche

Preparation time: 15 minutes

Cooking time: 2 hours

Servings: 11

Ingredients:

- Frozen spinach10 oz. package
- Butter or ghee1 tablespoon
- Red bell pepper1 medium
- Cheddar cheese1 1/2 cups
- Eggs8 pcs
- Homemade sour cream1 cup
- Fresh chives2 tablespoons
- Sea salt1/2 teaspoon
- Ground black pepper1/4 teaspoon
- Ground almond flour   1/2 cup
- Baking soda1/4 teaspoon

Directions:

1. Let the frozen spinach thaw and drain it well. Chop finely. Wash the pepper and slice it. Remove the seeds.
2. Grate the cheddar cheese and set aside. Chop the fresh chives finely.
3. Grease the slow cooker with cooking spray.
4. Take a little skillet, heat the butter over high heat on the stove, sauté the pepper until tender, for about 6 minutes. Mix the eggs, sour cream, salt, plus pepper in a large bowl.
5. Add grated cheese and chives and continue to mix. In another medium-sized bowl, combine almond flour with baking soda.
6. Pour into the egg mixture, add peppers to the egg's mixture, and pour gently into the slow cooker.
7. Set to cook on high within 2 hours then Serve.

Nutrition:

Calories: 153

Carbs: 19g

Fat: 3g

Protein: 9g

21.   Broccoli Gratin with Parmesan and Swiss Cheese

Preparation time: 15 minutes

Cooking time: 1 hour

Servings: 7

Ingredients:

- bite-size broccoli flowerets8 cups
- Swiss cheese1 1/2 cups

- mayo 8 teaspoon
- lemon juice1 1/2 tablespoon
- Dijon mustard3/4 teaspoon
- green onions3 tablespoon
- Parmesan cheese1/4 cup
- black pepper and salt to taste

Directions:

1. Wash broccoli and cut into small florets. Grate both parmesan and Swiss cheese into a bowl. Set aside.
2. Squeeze juice of a lemon into a cup. Wash and chop the green onions.
3. Grease with cooking spray or olive oil (optional) over the bottom of the slow cooker.
4. Put broccoli florets in a single layer. Mix in a separate bowl lemon juice, mustard, mayo, black pepper, add to the mixture green onion and grated cheese.
5. Put the mixture over the broccoli, cover, and cook on low 1 hour. Serve hot.

Nutrition:

Calories: 210

Carbs: 44g

Fat: 2g

Protein: 5g

22.   Crock Pot Cream Cheese French Toast

Preparation time: 15 minutes

Cooking time: 2 hours

Servings: 9

Ingredients:

- cream cheese 1 (8-oz) package
- slivered almonds ¼ cup
- keto bread 1 loaf
- eggs 4 pcs
- almond extract 1 teaspoon
- sweetener 1 tablespoon
- milk 1 cup
- butter 2 tablespoon
- Cheddar cheese ½ cup
- Maple syrup, at will, for dressing

Directions:

1. Mix cream cheese with almonds in a large bowl. Slice the keto bread into 2-inch slices. Try to make a 1/2-inch slit (horizontal) at the bottom of every piece to make a pocket.
2. Fill all the slices with cream mixture. Set aside. In a little bowl, mix eggs, extract the sweetener in milk. Coat the keto slices into the mix.
3. Grease with cooking spray the slow cooker over the bottom and sides, then put the coated keto slices on the slow cooker's base. Put on the top of each separate piece additional shredded cheese.
4. Cook on low for 2 hours. Serve hot.

Nutrition:

Calories: 280

Carbs: 34g

Fat: 8g

Protein: 19g

23. Keto Crock Pot Turkey Stuffed Peppers

Preparation time: 15 minutes

Cooking time: 6 hours

Servings: 7

Ingredients:

- olive oil1 tablespoon
- Ground turkey1 lb.
- onion1 pcs
- garlic1 clove
- green bell peppers4 pcs
- tomato sauce/pasta sauce (low carb)24 oz. jar
- water1/2 cup

Directions:

1. Peel and cut the small onion, peel the garlic, and press or mince it.
2. Wash the bell peppers, cut off the tops and clean them accurately.
3. Take a medium bowl, put their ground turkey, cut onion, pressed or minced garlic, and add pasta sauce.
4. Separate the compound into four equal parts, place the mixtures into the prepared cleaned peppers.
5. Spread the olive oil over the slow cooker bottom, and sides put the peppers inside, and top them with sauce.
6. Add a little water into the slow cooker, cook on low for 6-7 hours.
7. Serve with remaining sauce and enjoy.

Nutrition:

Calories: 245

Carbs: 26g

Fat: 7g

Protein: 19g

Chapter 6.   Lunch

24.   Lunch Chicken Wraps

Preparation time: 18 minutes

Cooking time: 6 hours

Servings: 6

Ingredients:

- 6 tortillas
- 3 tablespoon Caesar dressing
- 1-pound chicken breast
- ½ cup lettuce
- 1 cup water
- 1 oz. bay leaf
- 1 teaspoon salt
- 1 teaspoon ground pepper
- 1 teaspoon coriander
- 4 oz. Feta cheese

Directions:

1. Put the chicken breast in the slow cooker.
2. Sprinkle the meat with the bay leaf, salt, ground pepper, and coriander.
3. Add water and cook the chicken breast for 6 hours on LOW.
4. Then remove the cooked chicken from the slow cooker and shred it with a fork.

5. Chop the lettuce roughly.

6. Then chop Feta cheese. Combine the chopped **Ingredients:** together and add the shredded chicken breast and Caesar dressing.

7. Mix everything together well. After this, spread the tortillas with the shredded chicken mixture and wrap them. Enjoy!

Nutrition:

Calories 376,

Fat 18.5,

Fiber 3,

Carbs 29.43,

Protein 23

25. Nutritious Lunch Wraps

Preparation time: 20 minutes

Cooking time: 4 hours

Servings: 5

Ingredients:

- 7 oz. ground pork
- 5 tortillas
- 1 tablespoon tomato paste
- ½ cup onion, chopped
- ½ cup lettuce
- 1 teaspoon ground black pepper
- 1 teaspoon salt

- 1 teaspoon sour cream

- 5 tablespoons water

- 4 oz. Parmesan, shredded

- 2 tomatoes

Directions:

1. Combine the ground pork with the tomato paste, ground black pepper, salt, and sour cream. Transfer the meat mixture to the slow cooker and cook on HIGH for 4 hours.

2. Meanwhile, chop the lettuce roughly. Slice the tomatoes.

3. Place the sliced tomatoes in the tortillas and add the chopped lettuce and shredded Parmesan. When the ground pork is cooked, chill to room temperature.

4. Add the ground pork in the tortillas and wrap them. Enjoy!

Nutrition:

Calories 318,

Fat 7,

Fiber 2,

Carbs 3.76,

Protein 26

26. **Butternut Squash Soup**

Preparation time: 10 minutes

Cooking time: 8 hours

Servings: 9

Ingredients:

- 2-pound butternut squash
- 4 teaspoon minced garlic
- ½ cup onion, chopped
- 1 teaspoon salt
- ¼ teaspoon ground nutmeg
- 1 teaspoon ground black pepper
- 8 cups chicken stock
- 1 tablespoon fresh parsley

Directions:

1. Peel the butternut squash and cut it into the chunks.
2. Toss the butternut squash in the slow cooker.
3. Add chopped onion, minced garlic, and chicken stock.
4. Close the slow cooker lid and cook the soup for 8 hours on LOW.
5. Meanwhile, combine the ground black pepper, ground nutmeg, and salt together.
6. Chop the fresh parsley.
7. When the time is done, remove the soup from the slow cooker and blend it with a blender until you get a creamy soup.
8. Sprinkle the soup with the spice mixture and add chopped parsley. Serve the soup warm. Enjoy!

Nutrition:

Calories 129,

Fat 2.7,

Fiber 2,

Carbs 20.85,

Protein 7

27. Eggplant Bacon Wraps

Preparation time: 17 minutes

Cooking time: 5 hours

Servings: 6

Ingredients:

- 10 oz. eggplant, sliced into rounds

- 5 oz. halloumi cheese

- 1 teaspoon minced garlic

- 3 oz. bacon, chopped

- ½ teaspoon ground black pepper

- 1 teaspoon salt

- 1 teaspoon paprika

- 1 tomato

Directions:

1. Rub the eggplant slices with the ground black pepper, salt, and paprika.

2. Slice halloumi cheese and tomato.

3. Combine the chopped bacon and minced garlic together.

4. Place the sliced eggplants in the slow cooker. Cook the eggplant on HIGH for 1 hour.

5. Chill the eggplant. Place the sliced tomato and cheese on the eggplant slices.

6. Add the chopped bacon mixture and roll up tightly.

7. Secure the eggplants with the toothpicks and return the eggplant wraps back into the slow cooker. Cook the dish on HIGH for 4 hours more.

8. When the dish is done, serve it immediately. Enjoy!

Nutrition:

Calories 131,

Fat 9.4,

Fiber 2,

Carbs 7.25,

Protein 6

28.   Mexican Warm Salad

Preparation time: 26 minutes

Cooking time: 10 hours

Servings: 10

Ingredients:

- 1 cup black beans

- 1 cup sweet corn, frozen

- 3 tomatoes

- ½ cup fresh dill

- 1 chili pepper

- 7 oz. chicken fillet

- 5 oz. Cheddar cheese

- 4 tablespoons mayonnaise

- 1 teaspoon minced garlic

- 1 cup lettuce

- 5 cups chicken stock

- 1 cucumber

Directions:

1. Put the chicken fillet, sweet corn, black beans, and chicken stock in the slow cooker.

2. Close the slow cooker lid and cook the mixture on LOW for 10 hours.

3. When the time is done remove the mixture from the slow cooker.

4. Shred the chicken fillet with 2 forks. Chill the mixture until room temperature.

5. Chop the lettuce roughly. Chop the cucumber and tomatoes.

6. Place the lettuce, cucumber, and tomatoes on a large serving plate.

7. After this, shred Cheddar cheese and chop the chili pepper.

8. Add the chili pepper to the serving plate too.

9. After this, add the chicken mixture on the top of the salad.

10. Sprinkle the salad with the mayonnaise, minced garlic, and shredded cheese. Enjoy the salad immediately.

Nutrition:

Calories 182,

Fat 7.8,

Fiber 2,

Carbs 19.6,

Protein 9

29. Hot Chorizo Salad

Preparation time: 20 minutes

Cooking time: 4 hours 30 minutes

Servings: 6

Ingredients:

- 8 oz. chorizo
- 1 teaspoon olive oil
- 1 teaspoon cayenne pepper
- 1 teaspoon chili flakes
- 1 teaspoon ground black pepper
- 1 teaspoon onion powder
- 2 garlic cloves
- 3 tomatoes
- 1 cup lettuce
- 1 cup fresh dill
- 1 teaspoon oregano
- 3 tablespoons crushed cashews

Directions:

1. Chop the chorizo sausages roughly and place them in the slow cooker.

2. Cook the sausages for 4 hours on HIGH.

3. Meanwhile, combine the cayenne pepper, chili flakes, ground black pepper, and onion powder together in a shallow bowl.

4. Chop the tomatoes roughly and add them to the slow cooker after 4 hours. Cook the mixture for 30 minutes more on HIGH.

5. Chop the fresh dill and combine it with oregano.

6. When the chorizo sausage mixture is cooked, place it in a serving bowl. Tear the lettuce and add it in the bowl too.

7. After this, peel the garlic cloves and slice them.

8. Add the sliced garlic cloves in the salad bowl too.

9. Then sprinkle the salad with the spice mixture, olive oil, fresh dill mixture, and crush cashew. Mix the salad carefully. Enjoy!

Nutrition:

Calories 249,

Fat 19.8,

Fiber 2,

Carbs 7.69,

Protein 11

30.   Stuffed Eggplants

Preparation time: 20 minutes

Cooking time: 8 hours

Servings: 4

Ingredients:

- 4 medium eggplants
- 1 cup rice, half cooked
- ½ cup chicken stock
- 1 teaspoon salt
- 1 teaspoon paprika
- ½ cup fresh cilantro
- 3 tablespoons tomato sauce
- 1 teaspoon olive oil

Directions:

1. Wash the eggplants carefully and remove the flesh from them.
2. Then combine the rice with the salt, paprika, and tomato sauce.
3. Chop the fresh cilantro and add it to the rice mixture.
4. Then fill the prepared eggplants with the rice mixture.
5. Pour the chicken stock and olive oil in the slow cooker.
6. Add the stuffed eggplants and close the slow cooker lid.
7. Cook the dish on LOW for 8 hours. When the eggplants are done, chill them little and serve immediately. Enjoy!

Nutrition:

Calories 277,

Fat 9.1,

Fiber 24,

Carbs 51.92,

Protein 11

31.   Light Lunch Quiche

Preparation time: 21 minutes

Cooking time: 4 hours 25 minutes

Servings: 7

Ingredients:

- 7 oz. pie crust

- ¼ cup broccoli

- 1/3 cup sweet peas

- ¼ cup heavy cream

- 2 tablespoons flour

- 3 eggs

- 4 oz. Romano cheese, shredded

- 1 teaspoon cilantro

- 1 teaspoon salt

- ¼ cup spinach

- 1 tomato

Directions:

1. Cover the inside of the slow cooker bowl with parchment.

2. Put the pie crust inside and flatten it well with your fingertips.

3. Chop the broccoli and combine it with sweet peas. Combine the heavy cream, flour, cilantro, and salt together. Stir the liquid until smooth.

4. Then beat the eggs into the heavy cream liquid and mix it with a hand mixer. When you get a smooth mix, combine it with the broccoli.

5. Chop the spinach and add it to the mix. Chop the tomato and add it to the mix too. Pour the prepared mixture into the pie crust slowly.

6. Close the slow cooker lid and cook the quiche for 4 hours on HIGH.

7. After 4 hours, sprinkle the quiche surface with the shredded cheese and cook the dish for 25 minutes more. Serve the prepared quiche! Enjoy!

Nutrition:

Calories 287,

Fat 18.8,

Fiber 1,

Carbs 17.1,

Protein 11

32. Chicken Open Sandwich

Preparation time: 15 minutes

Cooking time: 8 hours

Servings: 4

Ingredients:

- 7 oz. chicken fillet

- 1 teaspoon cayenne pepper

- 5 oz. mashed potato, cooked

- 6 tablespoons chicken gravy

- 4 slices French bread, toasted

- 2 teaspoons mayo

- 1 cup water

Directions:

1. Put the chicken fillet in the slow cooker and sprinkle it with the cayenne pepper.

2. Add water and chicken gravy. Close the slow cooker lid and cook the chicken for 8 hours on LOW. Then combine the mashed potato with the mayo sauce.

3. Spread toasted French bread with the mashed potato mixture.

4. When the chicken is cooked, cut it into the strips and combine with the remaining gravy from the slow cooker.

5. Place the chicken strips over the mashed potato. Enjoy the open sandwich warm!

Nutrition:

Calories 314,

Fat 9.7,

Fiber 3,

Carbs 45.01,

Protein 12

33.   Onion Lunch Muffins

Preparation time: 15 minutes

Cooking time: 8 hours

Servings: 7

Ingredients:

- 1 egg

- 5 tablespoons butter, melted

- 1 cup flour

- ½ cup milk

- 1 teaspoon baking soda

- 1 cup onion, chopped

- 1 teaspoon cilantro

- ½ teaspoon sage

- 1 teaspoon apple cider vinegar

- 2 cup water

- 1 tablespoon chives

- 1 teaspoon olive oil

Directions:

1. Beat the egg in the bowl and add melted butter.

2. Add the flour, baking soda, chopped onion, milk, sage, apple cider vinegar, cilantro, and chives. Knead into a dough.

3. After this, spray a muffin form with the olive oil inside. Fill the ½ part of every muffin form and place them in the glass jars.

4. After this, pour water in the slow cooker vessel.

5. Place the glass jars with muffins in the slow cooker and close the lid.

6. Cook the muffins for 8 hours on LOW.

7. Check if the muffins are cooked with the help of the toothpick and remove them from the slow cooker. Enjoy the dish warm!

Nutrition:

Calories 180,

Fat 11,

Fiber 1,

Carbs 16.28,

Protein 4

34.   Tuna in Potatoes

Preparation time: 16 minutes

Cooking time: 4 hours

Servings: 8

Ingredients:

- 4 large potatoes

- 8 oz. tuna, canned

- ½ cup cream cheese

- 4 oz. Cheddar cheese

- 1 garlic clove

- 1 teaspoon onion powder

- ½ teaspoon salt

- 1 teaspoon ground black pepper

- 1 teaspoon dried dill

Directions:

1. Wash the potatoes carefully and cut them into the halves.

2. Wrap the potatoes in the foil and place in the slow cooker. Close the slow cooker lid and cook the potatoes on HIGH for 2 hours.

3. Meanwhile, peel the garlic clove and mince it. Combine the minced garlic clove with the cream cheese, tuna, salt, ground black pepper, onion powder, and dill.

4. Then shred Cheddar cheese and add it to the mixture.

5. Mix it carefully until homogenous.

6. When the time is over – remove the potatoes from the slow cooker and discard the foil only from the flat surface of the potatoes.

7. Then take the fork and mash the flesh of the potato halves gently. Add the tuna mixture in the potato halves and return them back in the slow cooker.

8. Cook the potatoes for 2 hours more on HIGH. Enjoy!

Nutrition:

Calories 247,

Fat 5.9,

Fiber 4,

Carbs 35.31,

Protein 14

35.   Banana Lunch Sandwiches

Preparation time: 15 minutes

Cooking time: 2 hours

Servings: 4

Ingredients:

- 2 banana

- 8 oz. French toast slices, frozen

- 1 tablespoon peanut butter

- ¼ teaspoon ground cinnamon

- 5 oz. Cheddar cheese, sliced

- ¼ teaspoon turmeric

Directions:

1. Peel the bananas and slice them.

2. Spread the French toast slices with the peanut butter well. Combine the ground cinnamon with the turmeric and stir the mixture. Sprinkle the French toasts with the spice mixture.

3. Then make the layer of the sliced bananas on the toasts and add the sliced cheese.

4. Cover the toast with the second part of the toast to make the sandwich.

5. Place the banana sandwiches in the slow cooker and cook them on HIGH for 2 hours.

6. Serve the prepared banana sandwiches hot. Enjoy!

Nutrition:

Calories 248,

Fat 7.5,

Fiber 2,

Carbs 36.74,

Protein 10

36. Parmesan Potato with Dill

Preparation time: 17 minutes

Cooking time: 4 hours

Servings: 5

Ingredients:

- 1-pound small potato

- ½ cup fresh dill

- 7 oz. Parmesan

- 1 teaspoon rosemary

- 1 teaspoon thyme

- 1 cup water

- ¼ teaspoon chili flakes

- 3 tablespoon cream

- 1 teaspoon salt

Directions:

1. Peel the potatoes and put them in the slow cooker.

2. Add water, salt, thyme, rosemary, and chili flakes.

3. Close the slow cooker lid and cook the potato for 2 hours on HIGH.

4. Meanwhile, shred Parmesan cheese and chop the fresh dill. When the time is done, sprinkle the potato with the cream and fresh dill. Stir it carefully.

5. Add shredded Parmesan cheese and close the slow cooker lid. Cook the potato on HIGH for 2 hours more.

6. Then open the slow cooker lid and do not stir the potato anymore. Gently transfer the dish to the serving plates. Enjoy!

Nutrition:

Calories 235,

Fat 3.9,

Fiber 2,

Carbs 32.26,

Protein 1

37.   Light Taco Soup

Preparation time: 24 minutes

Cooking time: 7 hours

Servings: 5

Ingredients:

- 7 oz. ground chicken

- ½ teaspoon sesame oil

- 3 cup vegetable stock

- 3 oz. yellow onion

- 1 cup tomato, canned

- 3 tomatoes

- 5 oz. corn kernels

- 1 jalapeno pepper, sliced

- ½ cup white beans, drained

- 3 tablespoon taco seasoning

- ¼ teaspoon salt

- 3 oz. black olives, sliced

- 5 corn tortillas, for serving

Directions:

1. Peel the onion and dice it. Chop the fresh and canned tomatoes.

2. Place the ground chicken, sesame oil, vegetable stock, diced onion, chopped tomatoes, sliced black olives, sliced jalapeno pepper, and corn in the slow cooker.

3. Add the white beans, taco seasoning, and salt.

4. Stir the soup mixture gently and close the slow cooker lid.

5. Cook the soup for 7 hours on LOW. Meanwhile, cut the corn tortillas into the strips and bake them in the preheated to 365 F oven for 10 minutes.

6. When the soup is cooked, ladle it into the serving bowls and sprinkle with the baked corn tortilla strips. Enjoy!

Nutrition:

Calories 328,

Fat 9.6,

Fiber 10,

Carbs 45.19,

Protein 18

38.   Slow Cooker Risotto

Preparation time: 20 minutes

Cooking time: 3 hours 30 minutes

Servings: 6

Ingredients:

- 7 oz. Parmigiano-Reggiano
- 2 cup chicken broth
- 1 teaspoon olive oil
- 1 onion, chopped
- ½ cup green peas
- 1 garlic clove, peeled and sliced
- 2 cups long grain rice
- ¼ cup dry wine
- 1 teaspoon salt
- 1 teaspoon ground black pepper
- 1 carrot, chopped
- 1 cup beef broth

Directions:

1. Spray a skillet with olive oil.

2. Add the chopped onion and carrot and roast the vegetables for 3 minutes on the medium heat. Then put the seared vegetables in the slow cooker. Toss the long grain rice in the remaining oil and sauté for 1 minute on the high heat.

3. Add the roasted long grain rice and sliced garlic in the slow cooker.

4. Add green peas, dry wine, salt, ground black pepper, and beef broth. After this, add the chicken broth and stir the mixture gently. Close the slow cooker lid and cook the risotto for 3 hours.

5. Then stir the risotto gently.

6. Shred Parmigiano-Reggiano and sprinkle over the risotto. Close the slow cooker lid and cook the dish for 30 minutes more. Enjoy the prepared risotto immediately!

Nutrition:

Calories 268,

Fat 3,

Fiber 4,

Carbs 53.34,

Protein 7

39.   Lemon Orzo

Preparation time: 20 minutes

Cooking time: 2 hours 30 minutes

Servings: 5

Ingredients:

- 4 oz. shallot

- 7 oz. orzo

- 2 cup chicken stock

- 1 teaspoon paprika

- 1 teaspoon ground black pepper

- 1 teaspoon salt

- 1 lemon

- ¼ cup cream

- 2 yellow sweet pepper

- 1 cup baby spinach

Directions:

1. Chop the shallot and place it in the slow cooker.

2. Add the chicken stock and paprika. Sprinkle the mixture with the ground black pepper and salt. Stir it gently and cook on HIGH for 30 minutes.

3. Meanwhile, grate the zest from the lemon and squeeze the juice. Add the lemon zest and juice in the slow cooker and stir it. After this, chop the baby spinach.

4. Add it into the slow cooker. Remove the seeds from the yellow sweet peppers and chop into tiny pieces. Add the chopped peppers to the slow cooker.

5. Add orzo and heavy cream. Stir the mass carefully and close the slow cooker lid. Cook the dish for 2 hours on LOW. Mix the dish gently. Enjoy!

Nutrition:

Calories 152,

Fat 4,

Fiber 3,

Carbs 24.79,

40.   Veggie Bean Stew

Preparation time: 20 minutes

Cooking time: 7 hours

Servings: 8

Ingredients:

- ½ cup barley

- 1 cup black beans

- ¼ cup red beans

- 2 carrots

- 1 cup onion, chopped

- 1 cup tomato juice

- 2 potatoes

- 1 teaspoon salt

- 1 teaspoon ground black pepper

- 4 cups water

- 4 oz. tofu

- 1 teaspoon garlic powder

- 1 cup fresh cilantro

Directions:

1. Place barley, black beans, and red beans in the slow cooker vessel.

2. Add chopped onion, tomato juice, salt, ground black pepper, and garlic powder. After this, add water and close the slow cooker lid.

3. Cook the dish for 4 hours on HIGH.

4. Meanwhile, peel the carrots and cut them into the strips. Peel the potatoes and chop.

5. Add the carrot strips and chopped potatoes in the slow cooker after 4 hours of cooking.

6. Chop the fresh cilantro and add it in the slow cooker too.

7. Stir the mix and close the slow cooker lid. Cook the stew for 3 hours more on LOW.

8. Serve the prepared dish immediately or keep it in the fridge, not more than 3 days. Enjoy!

Nutrition:

Calories 207,

Fat 3.5,

Fiber 8,

Carbs 37.67,

Protein 8

41.   Carrot Soup with Cardamom

Preparation time: 18 minutes

Cooking time: 12 hours

Servings: 9

Ingredients:

- 1-pound carrot

- 1 teaspoon ground cardamom

- ¼ teaspoon nutmeg

- 1 teaspoon salt

- 3 tablespoons fresh parsley

- 1 teaspoon honey

- 1 teaspoon marjoram

- 5 cups chicken stock

- ½ cup yellow onion, chopped

- 1 teaspoon butter

Directions:

1. Toss the butter in a pan and add chopped onion.

2. Chop the carrot and add it to the pan too.

3. Roast the vegetables for 5 minutes on the low heat. After this, place the roasted vegetables in the slow cooker. Add ground cardamom, nutmeg, salt, marjoram, and chicken stock.

4. Close the slow cooker lid and cook the soup for 12 hours on LOW.

5. Chop the fresh parsley.

6. When the time is over, blend the soup with a hand blender until you get a smooth texture. Then ladle the soup into the serving bowls.

7. Sprinkle the prepared soup with the chopped fresh parsley and honey. Enjoy the soup immediately!

Nutrition:

Calories 80,

Fat 2.7,

Fiber 2,

Carbs 10.19,

Protein 4

42.   Cod Chowder

Preparation time: 20 minutes

Cooking time: 3 hours

Servings: 6

Ingredients:

- 1 yellow onion
- 10 oz. cod
- 3 oz. bacon, sliced
- 1 teaspoon sage
- 5 oz. potatoes
- 1 carrot, grated
- 5 cups water
- 1 tablespoon almond milk
- 1 teaspoon ground coriander
- 1 teaspoon salt

Directions:

1. Peel the onion and chop it.

2. Put the chopped onion and grated carrot in the slow cooker bowl. Add the sage, almond milk, ground coriander, and water. After this, chop the cod into the 6 pieces.

3. Add the fish in the slow cooker bowl too. Then chop the sliced bacon and peel the potatoes.

4. Cut the potatoes into the cubes.

5. Add the Ingredients: in the slow cooker bowl and close the slow cooker lid.

6. Cook the chowder for 3 hours on HIGH. Ladle the prepared cod chowder in the serving bowls.

7. Sprinkle the dish with the chopped parsley if desired. Enjoy!

Nutrition:

Calories 108,

Fat 4.5,

Fiber 2,

Carbs 8.02,

Protein 10

43.   Sweet Corn Pilaf

Preparation time: 21 minutes

Cooking time: 8 hours

Servings: 5

Ingredients:

- 2 cups rice

- 1 cup sweet corn, frozen

- 6 oz. chicken fillet

- 1 sweet red pepper

- 1 yellow sweet pepper

- ½ cup green peas, frozen

- 1 carrot

- 4 cups chicken stock

- 2 tablespoon chopped almonds

- 1 teaspoon olive oil

- 1 teaspoon salt

- 1 teaspoon ground white pepper

Directions:

1. Peel the carrot and cut into the small cubes.

2. Combine the carrot cubes with the frozen sweet corn and green peas.

3. After this, place the vegetable mixture in the slow cooker vessel.

4. Add the rice, chicken stock, olive oil, salt, and ground white pepper.

5. After this, cut the chicken fillet into the strips and add the meat to the rice mixture.

6. Chop all the sweet peppers and add them in the slow cooker too.

7. Close the slow cooker lid and cook the pilaf for 8 hours on LOW.

8. When the pilaf is cooked, stir it gently and sprinkle with the almonds. Mix the dish carefully again. Serve it immediately. Enjoy!

Nutrition:

Calories 390,

Fat 18.6,

Fiber 13,

Carbs 54.7,

Protein 18

44.   Mediterranean Vegetable Mix

Preparation time: 15 minutes

Cooking time: 7 hours

Servings: 8

Ingredients:

- 1 zucchini
- 2 eggplants
- 2 red onion
- 4 potatoes
- 4 oz. asparagus
- 2 tablespoon olive oil
- 1 teaspoon ground black pepper
- 1 teaspoon paprika
- 1 teaspoon salt
- 1 tablespoon Mediterranean seasoning
- 1 teaspoon minced garlic

Directions:

1. Combine the olive oil, Mediterranean seasoning, salt, paprika, ground black pepper, and minced garlic together.

2. Whisk the mixture well. Wash all the vegetables carefully.

3. Cut the zucchini, eggplants, and potatoes into the medium cubes. Cut the asparagus into 2 parts.

4. Then peel the onions and cut them into 4 parts. Toss all the vegetables in the slow cooker and sprinkle them with the spice mixture.

5. Close the slow cooker lid and cook the vegetable mix for 7 hours on LOW.

6. Serve the prepared vegetable mix hot. Enjoy!

Nutrition:

Calories 227,

Fat 3.9,

Fiber 9,

Carbs 44.88,

Protein 6

45.   Spaghetti Cottage Cheese Casserole

Preparation time: 21 minutes

Cooking time: 7 hours

Servings: 8

Ingredients:

- 1-pound cottage cheese
- 7 oz. spaghetti, cooked
- 5 eggs
- 1 cup heavy cream
- 5 tablespoons semolina
- 3 tablespoons white sugar

- 1 teaspoon vanilla extract

- 1 teaspoon marjoram

- 1 teaspoon lemon zest

- 1 teaspoon butter

Directions:

1. Blend the cottage cheese in the blender for 1 minute to fluff.

2. Beat the eggs in the cottage mixture and continue to blend it for 3 minutes more on medium speed. Add the heavy cream, semolina, white sugar, vanilla extract, marjoram, lemon zest, and butter. Blend the mixture on the maximum speed for 1 minute.

3. Then chopped the cooked spaghetti. Place 3 tablespoon of the cottage cheese mixture in the slow cooker to make the bottom layer.

4. After this, make a layer from the chopped cooked spaghetti.

5. Repeat the steps till you use all the chopped spaghetti.

6. Then spread the last layer of the spaghetti with the cottage cheese mixture and close the slow cooker lid. Cook the casserole for 7 hours on LOW.

7. When the casserole is cooked, it will have a light brown color. Serve it warm and enjoy!

Nutrition:

Calories: 302g,

Fat: 22g,

Carbs: 5g,

Protein: 34g,

46.   Meatballs with Coconut Gravy

Preparation time: 20 minutes

Cooking time: 7 hours

Servings: 8

Ingredients:

- 3 tablespoons coconut

- 1 tablespoon curry paste

- 1 teaspoon salt

- 1 cup heavy cream

- 1 tablespoon flour

- 1 teaspoon cayenne pepper

- 10 oz. ground pork

- 1 egg

- 1 tablespoon semolina

- ½ cup onion, chopped

- 1 teaspoon kosher salt

- 3 tablespoons bread crumbs

- 1 teaspoon ground black pepper

Directions:

1. Combine the coconut, curry paste, and salt together.

2. Add heavy cream and flour.

3. Whisk the mixture and pour in the slow cooker. Cook on the LOW for 1 hour.

4. Meanwhile, beat the egg in the big bowl and whisk.

5. Add the cayenne pepper, ground pork, semolina, chopped onion, kosher salt, bread crumbs, and ground black pepper. Mix well and then make the small balls from the meat mixture and place them in the slow cooker.

6. Coat the meatballs with the prepared coconut gravy and close the lid.

7. Cook the dish for 7 hours on LOW. When the meatballs are cooked, serve them only with the coconut gravy. Enjoy!

Nutrition:

Calories: 312g,

Fat: 22g,

Carbs: 5g,

Protein: 34g,

47.   Pulled Pork Salad

Preparation time: 15 minutes

Cooking time: 8 hours

Servings: 4

Ingredients:

- 1 avocado, chopped

- 1 tomato, chopped

- 1 cup lettuce, chopped

- 1 tablespoon olive oil

- ½ teaspoon chili flakes

- 7 oz. pork loin

- 1 cup water

- 1 bay leaf

- 1 teaspoon salt

- ¼ teaspoon peppercorns

Directions:

1. Place the pork loin in the slow cooker.

2. Add the water, bay leaf, salt, and peppercorns.

3. Add the chili flakes and close the lid.

4. Cook the pork loin for 8 hours on Low.

5. Meanwhile, mix the chopped avocado, tomato, and lettuce in a large salad bowl.

6. When the pork loin is cooked, remove it from the water and place it in a separate bowl.

7. Shred the pork loin with two forks.

8. Add the shredded pork loin into the salad bowl.

9. Stir the salad gently and sprinkle with the olive oil.

10. Enjoy!

Nutrition:

Calories: 302g,

Fat: 22g,

Carbs: 5g,

Protein: 34g,

48.   Fresh Dal

Preparation time: 15 minutes

Cooking time: 5 hours

Servings: 11

Ingredients:

- 1 teaspoon cumin
- 1 oz. mustard seeds
- 10 oz. lentils
- 1 teaspoon fennel seeds
- 7 cups water
- 6 oz. tomato, canned
- 4 oz. onion
- ½ teaspoon fresh ginger, grated
- 1 oz. bay leaf
- 1 teaspoon turmeric
- 1 teaspoon salt
- 2 cups rice

Directions:

1. Peel the onion. Chop the onion and tomatoes and place them in a slow cooker.

2. Combine the cumin, mustard seeds, and fennel seeds in a shallow bowl.

3. Add the bay leaf and mix. Sprinkle the vegetables in the slow cooker with the spice mixture.

4. Add salt, turmeric, and grated fresh ginger. Add rice and mix.

5. Add the lentils and water. Stir gently.

6. Then close the slow cooker lid and cook Dal for 5 hours on LOW.

7. When the dish is done, stir and transfer to serving plates. Enjoy!

Nutrition:

Calories: 102g,

Fat: 22g,

Carbs: 5g,

Protein: 34g,

49.   Garlic Pork Belly

Preparation time: 15 minutes

Cooking time: 7 hours

Servings: 8

Ingredients:

- 1-pound pork belly

- 4 garlic cloves, peeled

- 1 teaspoon peppercorns

- 2 tablespoons mustard

- ½ teaspoon salt

- 1 tablespoon butter

- 1 cup water

Directions:

1. Dice the garlic cloves and combine them with the peppercorns and mustard.

2. Add the salt and butter and stir.

3. Rub the pork belly with the prepared mixture well.

4. Place the pork belly in the slow cooker.

5. Add the water and close the lid.

6. Cook the pork belly for 7 hours on Low.

7. Slice the cooked pork belly and serve!

Nutrition:

Calories: 321g,

Fat: 22g,

Carbs: 5g,

Protein: 34g,

50.   Sesame Seed Shrimp

Preparation time: 20 minutes

Cooking time: 30 minutes

Servings: 4

Ingredients:

- 1-pound shrimp, peeled

- 2 tablespoons apple cider vinegar

- 1 teaspoon paprika

- 1 teaspoon sesame seeds

- ¼ cup water

- 3 tablespoons butter

Directions:

1. Sprinkle the shrimp with the apple cider vinegar.

2. Add paprika and stir the shrimp.

3. Let the shrimp marinade for 15 minutes.

4. Pour water into the slow cooker.

5. Add the butter and marinated shrimp.

6. Cook the shrimp for 30 minutes on High.

7. Transfer the shrimp to a serving bowl.

8. Mix together the remaining liquid and sesame seeds.

9. Sprinkle the shrimp with the sesame mixture and enjoy!

Nutrition:

Calories: 102g,

Fat: 22g,

Carbs: 5g,

Protein: 34g,

51.   Cod Fillet in Coconut Flakes

Preparation time: 20 minutes

Cooking time: 1 hour

Servings: 4

Ingredients:

- ¼ cup coconut flakes, unsweetened

- 1 egg, beaten

- ½ teaspoon salt

- 1 teaspoon ground black pepper

- 10 oz. cod fillets

- 1 tablespoon butter

- 3 tablespoons water

Directions:

1. Whisk the egg, combine it with the salt, and ground black pepper.

2. Place the cod fillets in the egg mixture and stir well.

3. Coat the egged cod fillets in the coconut flakes.

4. Add the butter to the slow cooker.

5. Add water and coated cod fillets.

6. Close the lid and cook the fish for 1 hour on High.

7. Then transfer the cod fillets onto a cutting board and cut them into servings.

8. Enjoy the cod fillet warm!

Nutrition:

Calories 268,

Fat 3,

Fiber 4,

Carbs 53.34,

Protein 7

52.   Chicken Liver Pate

Preparation time: 25 minutes

Cooking time: 2 hours

Servings: 6

Ingredients:

- 1-pound chicken liver
- 1 onion, chopped
- 2 cups water
- 1 teaspoon salt
- ¼ teaspoon ground nutmeg
- 2 tablespoons butter
- 1 bay leaf

Directions:

1. Place the chicken liver in the slow cooker.

2. Add chopped onion, water, salt, ground black pepper, and bay leaf.

3. Close the lid and cook the liver for 2 hours on High.

4. After this, strain the chicken liver, discarding the liquid, and place it in the blender.

5. Add butter and blend the mixture until smooth (approximately for 3 minutes at maximum speed).

6. Transfer the cooked pate into a bowl and let it cool in the freezer for 10 minutes.

7. Serve with keto bread!

Nutrition:

Calories 368,

Fat 3,

Fiber 4,

Carbs 53.34,

Protein 7

53.   Garlic Duck Breast

Preparation time: 20 minutes

Cooking time: 5 hours

Servings: 6

Ingredients:

- 11 oz. duck breast, boneless, skinless
- 4 garlic cloves, roughly diced
- 1 teaspoon rosemary
- 1 tablespoon butter
- ½ cup water
- 1 teaspoon chili flakes

Directions:

1. Make small cuts in the duck breast.
2. Sprinkle the duck breast with the rosemary and chili flakes.
3. Fill the cuts with the diced garlic.
4. Place the duck breast in the slow cooker.
5. Add butter and water and close the lid.

6. Cook the duck breast for 5 hours on Low.

7. When the duck breast is cooked, remove it from the slow cooker and let it rest for 10 minutes.

8. Slice the duck breast and serve!

Nutrition:

Calories 268,

Fat 3,

Fiber 4,

Carbs 53.34,

Protein 7

54.   Thyme Lamb Chops

Preparation time: 20 minutes

Cooking time: 7 hours

Servings: 2

Ingredients:

- 8 oz. lamb chops

- 1 teaspoon liquid stevia

- 1 teaspoon thyme

- 1 tablespoon olive oil

- ¼ cup water

- 1 bay leaf

- ¾ teaspoon ground cinnamon

- ½ onion, chopped

Directions:

1. Mix the liquid stevia, thyme, olive oil, and ground cinnamon.

2. Rub the lamb chops with the spice mixture.

3. Place the lamb chops in the slow cooker and add chopped onion and water.

4. Add the bay leaf and close the lid.

5. Cook the lamb chops for 7 hours on Low.

6. When the meat is cooked, serve it immediately!

Nutrition:

Calories 368,

Fat 3,

Fiber 4,

Carbs 53.34,

Protein 7

55.   Autumn Pork Stew

Preparation time: 30 minutes

Cooking time: 6 hours

Servings: 5

Ingredients:

- 1 eggplant, chopped

- 4 oz. white mushrooms, chopped

- 1 white onion, chopped

- 2 cups water

- ½ teaspoon clove

- ½ teaspoon salt

- ½ teaspoon cayenne pepper

- 8 oz. pork tenderloin

Directions:

1. Place the chopped eggplant, mushrooms, onion, and water in the slow cooker.

2. Chop the pork tenderloin roughly and sprinkle it with the cayenne pepper, salt, and clove.

3. Stir the meat and place it in the slow cooker too.

4. Close the lid and cook the stew for 6 hours on Low.

5. When the stew is cooked, let it rest for 20 minutes.

6. Enjoy!

Nutrition:

Calories 168,

Fat 3,

Fiber 4,

Carbs 53.34,

Protein 7

56. Handmade Sausage Stew

Preparation time: 25 minutes

Cooking time: 3 hours

Servings: 3

Ingredients:

- 7 oz. ground pork
- 1 egg yolk
- ½ teaspoon salt
- ½ teaspoon ground black pepper
- 7 oz. broccoli, chopped
- ½ cup water
- 1 tomato, chopped
- 1 teaspoon butter

Directions:

1. Mix the ground pork and yolk. Add salt and ground black pepper.
2. Stir the mixture and form small sausages with your hands.
3. Place the sausages in the slow cooker.
4. Add the chopped broccoli and water.
5. Add chopped tomato and butter.
6. Close the lid and cook the stew for 3 hours on High.
7. Place the cooked stew in bowls and enjoy!

Nutrition:

Calories 268,

Fat 3,

Fiber 4,

Carbs 53.34,

Protein 7

57.   Marinated Beef Tenderloin

Preparation time: 20 minutes

Cooking time: 6 hours

Servings: 6

Ingredients:

- 2 tablespoons butter
- 1-pound Beef Tenderloin
- 1 teaspoon minced garlic
- ½ teaspoon ground nutmeg
- 1 teaspoon turmeric
- 1 teaspoon paprika
- 1 tablespoon apple cider vinegar
- ½ teaspoon dried oregano
- 1 cup water

Directions:

1. Melt the butter and mix it up with the minced garlic, ground nutmeg, turmeric, paprika, apple cider vinegar, and dried oregano.

2. Whisk the mixture.

3. Rub the beef tenderloin with the spice mixture.

4. Place the beef tenderloin in the slow cooker and add the remaining spice mixture.

5. Add water and close the lid.

6. Cook the beef tenderloin for 8 hours on Low.

7. Chop the beef tenderloin and serve it!

Nutrition:

Calories 68,

Fat 3,

Fiber 4,

Carbs 53.34,

Protein 7

58. Chicken Liver Sauté

Preparation time: 20 minutes

Cooking time: 5 hours

Servings: 4

Ingredients:

- 10 oz. chicken liver

- 1 onion, chopped

- 2 tablespoons full-fat cream

- 5 oz. white mushrooms, chopped

- 1 cup water

- 1 tablespoon butter

- 1 teaspoon salt

- ½ teaspoon ground black pepper

Directions:

1. Place the chicken liver, onion, full-fat cream, mushrooms, water, butter, salt, and ground black pepper in the slow cooker and close the lid.

2. Cook the mixture for 5 hours on Low.

3. When the liver saute is cooked, let it rest for 10 minutes.

4. Enjoy!

Nutrition:

Calories 168,

Fat 3,

Fiber 4,

Carbs 53.34,

Protein 7

59.   Chicken in Bacon

Preparation time: 20 minutes

Cooking time: 3 hours

Servings: 6

Ingredients:

- 1-pound chicken thighs

- 7 oz. bacon, sliced

- 1 tablespoon butter

- ¾ cup water

- ½ teaspoon ground black pepper

- 1 teaspoon chili flakes

- 1 teaspoon paprika

Directions:

1. Sprinkle the chicken thighs with the ground black pepper, chili flakes, and paprika.

2. Wrap the chicken thighs in the sliced bacon and transfer to the slow cooker.

3. Add the water and butter and close the lid.

4. Cook the chicken for 3 hours on High.

5. Serve the cooked meal immediately!

Nutrition:

Calories 268,

Fat 3,

Fiber 4,

Carbs 53.34,

Protein 7

60.   Whole Chicken

Preparation time: 40 minutes

Cooking time: 10 hours

Servings: 10

Ingredients:

- 2-pound whole chicken

- 4 oz. celery stalk, chopped

- 1 onion, chopped

- 3 garlic cloves, peeled

- 1 tablespoon rosemary

- 1 teaspoon dried oregano

- 2 tablespoons butter

- 1 teaspoon salt

- ½ teaspoon ground coriander

- 1 teaspoon turmeric

- 2 cups water

Directions:

1. Rub the chicken with the rosemary, dried oregano, salt, ground coriander, and turmeric.

2. Fill the chicken cavity with the chopped celery, garlic cloves, onion, and butter.

3. Place the chicken in the slow cooker and add water.

4. Close the lid and cook the chicken for 10 hours on Low.

5. When the chicken is cooked, leave it for 20 minutes to rest.

6. Serve and enjoy!

Nutrition:

Calories 248,

Fat 7.5,

Fiber 2,

Carbs 36.74,

Protein 10

61. Duck Rolls

Preparation time: 25 minutes

Cooking time: 3 hours

Servings: 6

Ingredients:

- 2-pound duck fillets

- 1 teaspoon minced garlic

- 1 cup spinach, chopped

- ¼ cup water

- 1 teaspoon rosemary

- 1 tablespoon olive oil

Directions:

1. Beat the duck fillets gently to tenderize and flatten then sprinkle them with the minced garlic, rosemary, and olive oil.

2. Place the chopped spinach on each of the duck fillets and roll them up, enclosing the spinach inside the duck.

3. Secure the duck rolls with the toothpicks and place them in the slow cooker.

4. Add water and close the lid.

5. Cook the duck rolls for 3 hours on High.

6. Cool the rolls slightly and serve!

Nutrition:

Calories 248,

Fat 7.5,

Fiber 2,

Carbs 36.74,

Protein 10

62. Keto Adobo Chicken

Preparation time: 15 minutes

Cooking time: 2 hours

Servings: 4

Ingredients:

- 1-pound chicken breast, boneless, skinless
- 1 tablespoon soy sauce
- 1 tablespoon olive oil
- 1 tablespoon apple cider vinegar
- 1 teaspoon minced garlic

Directions:

1. Chop the chicken breast roughly and sprinkle it with the soy sauce, olive oil, apple cider vinegar, and minced garlic.

2. Mix and then let sit for 20 minutes to marinate.

3. Transfer the chicken and all the remaining liquid into the slow cooker.

4. Close the lid and cook the meal for 2 hours on High.

5. Enjoy!

Nutrition:

Calories 348,

Fat 7.5,

Fiber 2,

Carbs 36.74,

Protein 10

63.   Cayenne Pepper Drumsticks

Preparation time: 20 minutes

Cooking time: 5 hours

Servings: 2

Ingredients:

- 10 oz. chicken drumsticks

- 1 teaspoon cayenne pepper

- 1 bell pepper, chopped

- ½ cup water

- 1 tablespoon butter

- 1 teaspoon thyme

- 1 teaspoon cumin

- ½ teaspoon chili pepper

Directions:

1. Mix the cayenne pepper, chopped bell pepper, butter, thyme, cumin, and chili pepper.

2. Stir the mixture until smooth,

3. Rub the chicken drumsticks with the spice mixture and place them in the slow cooker.

4. Add water and close the lid.

5. Cook the drumsticks for 5 hours on Low.

6. Transfer the cooked meal onto a platter and serve!

Nutrition:

Calories 248,

Fat 7.5,

Fiber 2,

Carbs 36.74,

Protein 10

64.   Keto BBQ Chicken Wings

Preparation time: 20 minutes

Cooking time: 2 hours

Servings: 4

Ingredients:

- 1-pound chicken wings

- 1 teaspoon minced garlic

- 1 teaspoon cumin

- 1 teaspoon ground coriander

- 1 teaspoon dried dill

- 1 teaspoon dried parsley

- 1 tablespoon mustard

- 1 teaspoon liquid stevia

- 1 tablespoon tomato paste

- 1 teaspoon salt

- 1 tablespoon apple cider vinegar

Directions:

1. Mix the minced garlic, cumin, ground coriander, dried dill, dried parsley, mustard, liquid stevia, tomato paste, salt, and apple cider vinegar.

2. Stir the mixture until smooth.

3. Combine the spice mixture and chicken wings and stir well.

4. Transfer the chicken wings and all the remaining spice mixture into the slow cooker.

5. Close the lid and cook for 2 hours on High.

6. Cool the chicken wings slightly and serve!

Nutrition:

Calories 148,

Fat 7.5,

Fiber 2,

Carbs 36.74,

Protein 10

Chapter 7.   Dinner

65.   Pork Chops

Preparation time: 5 minutes

Cooking time: 6 hours

Servings: 8

Ingredients:

- 2 pounds pasture-raised pork chops
- 1 teaspoon salt
- 1 tablespoon dried thyme
- 1 tablespoon dried rosemary
- 1 tablespoon ground cumin
- 1 tablespoon dried curry powder
- 1 tablespoon chopped fresh chives
- 1 tablespoon fennel seeds
- 1 tablespoons avocado oil

Directions:

1. Place 2 tablespoons oil in a small bowl, add remaining **Ingredients:** except for pork, and stir until well mixed.
2. Rub this mixture on all sides of pork chops until evenly coated.
3. Grease a 6-quart slow cooker with remaining oil, add seasoned pork chops, and shut with lid.
4. Plug in the slow cooker and cook pork for 6 hours at a low heat setting or 4 hours at a high heat setting.
5. Serve straight away.

Nutrition:

Net Carbs: 1g

Calories: 235

Total Fat: 15g

Saturated Fat: 3g

Protein: 24g

Carbs: 1g

Fiber: 0g

Sugar: 0g

66.   Spicy Pork & Spinach Stew

Preparation time: 5 minutes

Cooking time: 4 hours and 20 minutes

Servings: 5

Ingredients:

- 1-pound pasture-raised pork butt, fat trimmed and cut into 2-inch pieces
- 4 cups chopped baby spinach
- 4 ounces Rotel tomatoes
- 1 large white onion, peeled and quartered
- cloves of garlic, peeled
- 1 teaspoon dried thyme
- 2 teaspoons Cajun seasoning blend

- 2 tablespoons avocado oil
- ¾ cup heavy whipping cream

Directions:

1. Place tomatoes, onion, and garlic in a food processor and pulse for 1 to 2 minutes or until blended.
2. Pour this mixture into a 6-quart slow cooker, add Cajun seasoning mix, thyme, avocado oil, and pork pieces, and stir well until evenly coated.
3. Plug in the slow cooker, then shut with lid and cook for 5 hours at low heat setting or 2 hours at high heat setting.
4. When done, stir in cream until combined, add spinach and continue cooking at low heat setting for 20 minutes or more until spinach wilts.
5. Serve straight away.

Nutrition:

Net Carbs: 3.3g

Calories: 604

Total Fat: 38.3g

Saturated Fat: 9g

Protein: 56g

Carbs: 9g

Fiber: 5g;

Sugar: 4g

67.   Stuffed Taco Peppers

Preparation time: 5 minutes

Cooking time: 8 hours

Servings: 6

Ingredients:

- 1 cup cauliflower rice
- 1 small red bell peppers
- 18-ounce minced pork, pasture-raised
- 1 teaspoon garlic powder
- ¾ teaspoon salt
- 1 teaspoon red chili powder
- 1 cup shredded Monterey jack cheese and more for topping
- 2 tablespoons avocado oil
- 1 cup water

Directions:

1. Remove and discard stem from each pepper and then scoop out seeds.
2. Place meat in a large bowl, add garlic, salt, and red chili powder, and stir until combined.

3. Then stir in cauliflower rice and oil until just combine and then stir in cheese.
4. Stuff this mixture into each pepper and place them in a 4-quart slow cooker.
5. Pour water into the bottom of the slow cooker, switch it on, and shut with the lid.
6. Cook peppers for 4 hours at high heat setting or 8 hours at low heating setting and top peppers with more cheese in the last 10 minutes of cooking time.
7. Serve straight away.

Nutrition:

Net Carbs: 4g

Calories: 270

Total Fat: 18g

Saturated Fat: 5g

Protein: 21g

Carbs: 6g

Fiber: 2g

Sugar: 3g

68. Lamb Barbacoa

Preparation time: 5 minutes

Cooking time: 8 hours

Servings: 12

Ingredients:

- 2 pounds pasture-raised pork shoulder, fat trimmed
- 2 tablespoons salt
- 1 teaspoon chipotle powder
- 2 tablespoons smoked paprika
- 1 tablespoon ground cumin
- 1 tablespoon dried oregano
- ¼ cup dried mustard
- 1 cup water

Directions:

1. Stir together salt, chipotle powder, paprika, cumin, oregano, and mustard and rub this mixture generously all over the pork.

2. Place seasoned pork into a 6-quart slow cooker, plug it in, then shut with lid and cook for 6 hours at high heat setting.
3. When done, shred pork with two forks and stir well until coated well.
4. Serve straight away.

Nutrition:

Net Carbs: 0.7g

Calories: 477

Total Fat: 35.8g

Saturated Fat: 14.8g

Protein: 37.5g

Carbs: 1.2g

Fiber: 0.5g

Sugar: 5g

69.   Pork Chile Verde

Preparation time: 5 minutes

Cooking time: 7 hours and 5 minutes

Servings: 6

Ingredients:

- 2 pounds pasture-raised pork shoulder, cut into 6 pieces
- 1 teaspoon sea salt
- ½ teaspoon ground black pepper
- 1 ½ tablespoon avocado oil
- 1 ½ cup salsa Verde
- 1 cup chicken broth

Directions:

1. Season pork with salt and black pepper.
2. Place a large skillet pan over medium heat, add oil, and when hot, add seasoned pork pieces.
3. Cook pork for 3 to 4 minutes per side or until browned and then transfer to a 6-quart slow cooker.
4. Whisk together salsa and chicken broth and pour over pork pieces.
5. Plug in the slow cooker, then shut with lid and cook for 6 to 7 hours at low heat setting or until pork is very tender.
6. When done, shred pork with two forks and stir until combined.

Nutrition :

Net Carbs: 4g

Calories : 342

Total Fat: 22g

Saturated Fat: 12g

Protein: 32g

Carbs: 6g

Fiber: 2g

Sugar: 4g

70.   Ham Soup

Preparation time: 5 minutes

Cooking time: 4 hours

Servings: 6

Ingredients:

- 2 pounds pasture-raised smoked ham hock
- 2 cups cauliflower florets
- 2 bay leaves
- ¼ teaspoon nutmeg
- cups bone broth

Directions:

1. Place cauliflower florets in a 6-quarts slow cooker, add remaining Ingredients, and pour in water until all the Ingredients are just submerged.
2. Plug in the slow cooker, then shut with lid and cook for 4 hours at high heat setting or until cauliflower florets are very tender.
3. Transfer ham to a bowl, shred with two forms, and discard bone and fat pieces.
4. Puree cauliflower in the slow cooker with a stick blender for 1 to 2 minutes or until smooth, return shredded ham, and stir until well combined.
5. Taste soup to adjust seasoning and serve.

Nutrition :

Net Carbs: 3g

Calories : 349

Total Fat: 23g

Saturated Fat: 10g

Protein: 34g

Carbs: 5g

Fiber: 2g

Sugar: 2g

71.   Minced Pork Zucchini Lasagna

Preparation time: 20 minutes

Cooking time: 8 hours

Servings: 4

Ingredients:

- medium zucchinis
- 1 diced small onion
- 1 minced clove of garlic
- 2 cups of minced lean ground pork
- 2 cans of Italian diced tomatoes
- 2 tablespoons of olive oil
- 2 cups of shredded Mozzarella cheese
- 1 large egg
- 1 tablespoon of dried basil
- Salt and pepper
- 2 tablespoons of butter

Directions:

1. Slice the zucchini lengthwise into 6 slices.
2. Heat the olive oil in a saucepan, and sauté the garlic and onions for 5 minutes.
3. Add the minced meat and cook for a further 5 minutes.
4. Add the tomatoes and cook for a further 5 minutes.
5. Add the seasoning and mix thoroughly.
6. In a small bowl, combine the egg and cheese and whisk together.
7. Use the butter to grease the crock pot and then begin to layer the lasagna.
8. First, layer with the zucchini slices, add the meat mixture, and then top with the cheese.
9. Repeat and finish with the cheese.

10. Cover and cook for 8 hours on low.

Nutrition:

Carbohydrates: 10 grams

Protein: 23 grams

Fat: 30 grams

Calories: 398

72. Beef Dijon

Preparation time: 15 minutes

Cooking time: 5 hours

Servings: 4

Ingredients:

- (6 oz.) small round steaks
- 2 tbsp. of each:
- Steak seasoning - to taste
- Avocado oil
- Peanut oil
- Balsamic vinegar/dry sherry
- tbsp. large chopped green onions/small chopped onions for the garnish - extra
- 1/4 c. whipping cream
- 1 c. fresh crimini mushrooms - sliced
- 1 tbsp. Dijon mustard

Directions:

1. Warm up the oils using the high heat setting on the stove top. Flavor each of the steaks with pepper and arrange to a skillet.
2. Cook two to three minutes per side until done.
3. Place into the slow cooker. Pour in the skillet drippings, half of the mushrooms, and the onions.
4. Cook on the low setting for four hours.
5. When the cooking time is done, scoop out the onions, mushrooms, and steaks to a serving platter.
6. In a separate dish - whisk together the mustard, balsamic vinegar, whipping cream, and the steak drippings from the slow cooker.
7. Empty the gravy into a gravy server and pour over the steaks.
8. Enjoy with some brown rice, riced cauliflower, or potatoes.

Nutrition:

Calories: 535

Net Carbs: 5.0 g

Fat: 40 g

Protein: 39 g

73.   Cabbage & Corned Beef

Preparation time: 10 minutes

Cooking time: 8 hours

Servings: 10

Ingredients:

- lb. corned beef
- 1 large head of cabbage
- c. water
- 1 celery bunch
- 1 small onion
- 4 carrots
- ½ t. of each:
- Ground mustard
- Ground coriander
- Ground marjoram
- Black pepper
- Salt
- Ground thyme
- Allspice

Directions:

1. Dice the carrots, onions, and celery and toss them into the cooker. Pour in the water.
2. Combine the spices, rub the beef, and arrange in the cooker. Secure the lid and cook on low for seven hours.
3. Remove the top layer of cabbage. Wash and cut it into quarters it until ready to cook. When the beef is done, add the cabbage, and cook for one hour on the low setting.
4. Serve and enjoy.

Nutrition:

Calories: 583

Net Carbs: 13 g

Fat: 40 g

Protein: 42 g

74.   Chipotle Barbacoa

Preparation time: 20 minutes

Cooking time: 4 hours

Servings: 9

Ingredients:

- ½ c. beef/chicken broth
- 2 med. chilies in adobo (with the sauce, it's about 4 teaspoons)
- lb. chuck roast/beef brisket
- minced garlic cloves
- 2 tbsp. of each:
- Lime juice
- Apple cider vinegar
- 2 t. of each:
- Sea salt
- Cumin
- 1 tbsp. dried oregano
- 1 t. black pepper
- 2 whole bay leaves
- Optional: ½ t. ground cloves

Directions:

1. Mix the chilies in the sauce, and add the broth, garlic, ground cloves, pepper, cumin, salt, vinegar, and lime juice in a blender, mixing until smooth.

2. Chop the beef into two-inch chunks and toss it in the slow cooker. Empty the puree on top. Toss in the two bay leaves.

3. Cook four to six hrs. On the high setting or eight to ten using the low setting.

4. Dispose of the bay leaves when the meat is done.

5. Shred and stir into the juices to simmer for five to ten minutes.

Nutrition:

Calories: 242

Net Carbs: 2 g

Fat: 11 g

Protein: 32 g

75.   Corned Beef Cabbage Rolls

Preparation time: 25 minutes

Cooking time: 6 hours

Servings: 5

Ingredients:

- ½ lb. corned beef
- large savoy cabbage leaves
- ¼ c. of each:
- White wine
- Coffee
- 1 large lemon
- 1 med. sliced onion
- 1 tbsp. of each:

- Rendered bacon fat
- Erythritol
- Yellow mustard

2 t. of each:

- Kosher salt
- Worcestershire sauce

¼ t. of each:

- Cloves
- Allspice
- 1 large bay leaf

1 t. of each:

- Mustard seeds
- Whole peppercorns
- ½ t. red pepper flakes

Directions:

1. Add the liquids, spices, and corned beef into the cooker. Cook six hours on the low setting.
2. Prepare a pot of boiling water.
3. When the time is up, add the leaves along with the sliced onion to the water for two to three minutes.
4. Transfer the leaves to a cold-water bath - blanching them for three to four minutes. Continue boiling the onion.
5. Use a paper towel to dry the leaves. Add the onions and beef. Roll up the cabbage leaves.
6. Drizzle with freshly squeezed lemon juice.

Nutrition:

Calories: 481.4

Net Carbs: 4.2 g

Protéine: 34.87 g

Fat: 25.38 g

76.   Cube Steak

Preparation time: 15 minutes

Cooking time: 8 hours

Servings: 8

Ingredients:

- Cubed steaks (28 oz.)
- 1 ¾ t. adobo seasoning/garlic salt
- 1 can (8 oz.) tomato sauce
- 1 c. water
- Black pepper to taste
- ½ med. onion
- 1 small red pepper
- 1/3 c. green pitted olives (+) 2 tbsp. brine

Directions:

1. Slice the peppers and onions into ¼-inch strips.
2. Sprinkle the steaks with the pepper and garlic salt as needed and place them in the cooker.

3. Fold in the peppers and onion along with the water, sauce, and olives (with the liquid/brine from the jar).
4. Close the lid. Prepare using the low-temperature setting for eight hours.

Nutrition :

Calories : 154

Net Carbs: 4 g

Protein: 23.5 g

Fat: 5.5 g

77.   Ragu

Preparation time: 10 minutes

Cooking time: 8 hours

Servings: 2

Ingredients:

- ¼ of each - diced:
- 4 Carrot
- Rib of celery
- 1 Onion
- 1 minced garlic clove
- ½ lb. top-round lean beef

(3 oz.) Of each:

- Diced tomatoes

- Crushed tomatoes
- 2 ½ t. beef broth (+) ¼ c.

1 ¼ t. of each:

- Chopped fresh thyme
- Minced fresh rosemary
- 1 bay leaf
- Pepper & Salt to taste

Directions:

1. Place the prepared celery, garlic, onion, and carrots into the slow cooker.
2. Trim away the fat and add the meat to the slow cooker. Sprinkle with the salt and pepper
3. Stir in the rest of the Ingredient.
4. Prepare on the low setting for six to eight hours. Enjoy any way you choose.

Nutrition:

Calories: 224

Net Carbs: 6 g

Protein: 27 g

Fat: 9 g

78.   Rope Vieja

Preparation time: 15 minutes

Cooking time: 8 hours

Servings: 6

Ingredients:

- 2 lb. flank steak – remove fat

1 of each:

- Yellow pepper
- Thinly sliced onion
- Green pepper
- Bay leaf
- ¼ t. salt

¾ t. of each:

- Oregano
- Non-fat beef broth
- Tomato paste
- Cooking spray

Directions:

1. Prepare the crockpot with the spray or use a liner and combine all of the fixings.
2. Stir everything together and prepare using low for eight hours.
3. Top it off with your chosen garnishes.

Nutrition:

Calories: 257

Net Carbs: 7 g

Fat: 10 g

Protein: 35 g

79.   Spinach Soup

Preparation time: 15 minutes

Cooking time: 6-8 hours

Servings: 4

Ingredients:

- 2 pounds spinach
- ¼ cup cream cheese
- 1 onion, diced
- 2 cups heavy cream
- 1 garlic clove, minced
- 2 cups water
- salt, pepper, to taste

Directions:

1. Pour water into the slow cooker. Add spinach, salt, and pepper.
2. Add cream cheese, onion, garlic, and heavy cream.
3. Close the lid and cook on Low for 6-8 hours.
4. Puree soup with blender and serve.

Nutrition:

Calories 322

Fats 28.2g

Net carbs 10.1g

Protein 12.2g

80.   Mashed Cauliflower with Herbs

Preparation time: 15 minutes

Cooking time: 3-6 hours

Servings: 4

Ingredients:

- 1 cauliflower head, cut into florets
- garlic cloves, peeled
- ½ teaspoon fresh rosemary, chopped
- ½ teaspoon fresh thyme, chopped
- ½ teaspoon fresh sage, chopped
- ½ teaspoon fresh parsley, chopped
- 1 cup vegetable broth
- 2 cups water
- 1 tablespoons ghee
- Salt, pepper, to taste

Directions:

1. Pour broth into the slow cooker, add cauliflower florets.
2. Add water, it should cover the cauliflower.
3. Close the lid and cook on Low for 6 hours or on High for 3 hours.
4. Once cooked, drain water from the slow cooker.
5. Add herbs, salt, and pepper, and ghee, puree with a blender.

Nutrition:

Calories 115

Fats 12g

Net carbs 4.7g

Protein 6.2g

81.   Kale Quiche

Preparation time: 15 minutes

Cooking time: 3-5 hours

Servings: 3

Ingredients:

- 1 cup almond milk
- 4 eggs
- 1 cup Carbquick Baking Mix
- 2 cups spinach, chopped
- ½ bell pepper, chopped
- cups fresh baby kale, chopped
- 1 teaspoon garlic, chopped
- 1/3 cup fresh basil, chopped
- salt, pepper, to taste
- 1 tablespoon olive oil

Directions:

1. Add oil to a slow cooker or use a cooking spray.
2. Beat eggs into a slow cooker; add almond milk and Baking Mix, mix to combine.
3. Add spinach, bell pepper, garlic, and basil, stir to combine.
4. Close the lid and cook on Low for 5 hours or on High for 3 hours.

5. Make sure the quiche is done, check the center with a toothpick, it should be dry.

Nutrition :

Calories 273

Fats 24.4g

Net carbs 5.8g

Protein 10.5g

82.　　　Spinach Stuffed Portobello

Preparation time: 15 minutes

Cooking time: 3 hours

Servings: 8

Ingredients:

- oz. medium-sized Portobello mushrooms, stems removed
- 1 tablespoons olive oil
- ½ onion, chopped
- 2 cups fresh spinach, rinsed and chopped
- garlic cloves, minced
- 1 cup chicken broth
- tablespoons parmesan cheese, grated
- 1/3 teaspoon dried thyme
- salt, pepper, to taste

Directions:

1. Heat oil in a medium pan over high heat. Add onion, cook until translucent, stirring steadily. Add spinach and thyme, cook for 1-2 minutes until spinach is wilted.
2. Brush each mushroom with olive oil.
3. Put 1 tablespoon of onion and spinach stuffing into each mushroom.
4. Pour chicken broth into a slow cooker. Put stuffed mushrooms on the bottom.
5. Close the lid and cook on High for 3 hours.
6. Once cooked, sprinkle mushrooms with parmesan cheese and serve.

Nutrition:

Calories 310g

Fats 21g

Net carbs 3g

Protein 12g

83.   Poached Salmon

Preparation time: 15 minutes

Cooking time: 1 hour

Servings: 4

Ingredients:

- medium salmon fillets
- water
- 2 tablespoons dry white wine

- 1 yellow onion, sliced
- ½ lemon, sliced
- ½ teaspoon salt
- ¼ teaspoon garlic powder
- ¼ teaspoon dried basil

Directions:

1. Pour water and wine into a slow cooker. Heat on High for 30 minutes with the lid open.
2. Season salmon fillets with salt, garlic powder, and basil.
3. Put salmon into a slow cooker. Add onion and lemon onto salmon fillets.
4. Close the lid and cook on High for 20-30 minutes.

Nutrition :

Calories 273

Fats 21g

Net carbs 4.2g

Protein 35g

84.   Cod and Vegetables

Preparation time: 15 minutes

Cooking time: 1-3 hours

Servings: 4

Ingredients:

- (5-6 oz.) cod fillets
- 1 bell pepper, sliced or chopped
- 1 onion, sliced
- ½ fresh lemon, sliced
- 1 zucchini, sliced
- garlic cloves, minced
- ¼ cup low-sodium broth
- 1 teaspoon rosemary
- ¼ teaspoon red pepper flakes
- Salt, pepper, to taste

Directions:

1. Season cod fillets with salt and pepper.
2. Pour broth into a slow cooker, add garlic, rosemary, bell pepper, onion, and zucchini into the slow cooker.
3. Put fish into your crockpot, add lemon slices on top.
4. Close the lid and cook on Low for 2-3 hours or on High for 1 hour.

Nutrition:

Calories 150

Fats 11.6g

Net carbs 6.2g

Protein 26.9g

85.   Balsamic Beef Pot Roast

Preparation time: 15 minutes

Cooking time: 4 hours

Servings: 10

Ingredients:

- 1 boneless (3 lb.) chuck roast
- 1 tbsp. of each:
- Kosher salt
- Black ground pepper
- Garlic powder
- ¼ c. balsamic vinegar
- ½ c. chopped onion
- 2 c. water
- ¼ t. xanthan gum
- For the Garnish: Fresh parsley

Directions:

1. Season the chuck roast with garlic powder, pepper, and salt over the entire surface.
2. Use a large skillet to sear the roast until browned.
3. Deglaze the bottom of the pot using balsamic vinegar. Cook one minute. Add to the slow cooker.
4. Mix in the onion and add the water. Once it starts to boil, secure the lid, and continue cooking on low for three to four hours.
5. Take the meat out of the slow cooker, and place it in a large bowl where you will break it up carefully into large chunks.
6. Remove all fat and anything else that may not be healthy such as too much fat.
7. Whisk the xanthan gum into the broth, and add it back to the slow cooker.

8. Serve and enjoy with a smile!

Nutrition :

Calories : 393

Net Carbs: 3 g

Protein: 30 g

86. Moist and Spicy Pulled Chicken Breast

Preparation time: 15 minutes

Cooking time: 6 hours

Servings: 8

Ingredients:

- 1 teaspoon dry oregano
- 1 teaspoon dry thyme
- 1 teaspoon dried rosemary
- 1 teaspoon garlic powder
- 1 teaspoon sweet paprika
- ½ teaspoon chili powder
- Salt and pepper to taste
- tablespoons butter
  - pounds of chicken breasts
- 1 ½ cups ready-made tomato salsa
- 2 Tablespoons of olive oil

Directions:

1. Mix dry seasoning, sprinkle half on the bottom of crockpot.
2. Place the chicken breasts over it, sprinkle the rest of the spices.
3. Pour the salsa over the chicken. Cover, cook on low for 6 hours.

Nutrition:

Calories: 42

Carbs: 1g

Fat: 1g

Protein: 9g

87.   Whole Roasted Chicken

Preparation time: 15 minutes

Cooking time: 8 hours

Servings: 6

Ingredients:

- 1 whole chicken (approximately 5.5 pounds)
- garlic cloves
- small onions
- 1 Tablespoon olive oil, for rubbing
- 2 teaspoons salt
- 2 teaspoons sweet paprika
- 1 teaspoon Cayenne pepper
- 1 teaspoon onion powder
- 1 teaspoon ground thyme
- 2 teaspoons fresh ground black pepper
- Tablespoons butter, cut into cubes

Directions:

1. Mix all dry **Ingredients:** well.
2. Stuff the chicken belly with garlic and onions.
3. On the bottom of the crockpot, place four balls of aluminum foil.
4. Set the chicken on top of the balls. Rub it generously with olive oil.
5. Cover the chicken with seasoning, drop in butter pieces. Cover, cook on low for 8 hours.

Nutrition:

Calories: 120

Carbs: 1g

Fat: 6g

Protein: 17g

88.   Pot Roast Beef Brisket

Preparation time: 15 minutes

Cooking time: 12 hours

Servings: 10

Ingredients:

- o pounds beef brisket, whole
- 2 Tablespoons olive oil
- 2 Tablespoons apple cider vinegar
- 1 teaspoon dry oregano
- 1 teaspoon dry thyme
- 1 teaspoon dried rosemary
- 2 Tablespoons paprika
- 1 teaspoon Cayenne pepper
- 1 tablespoon salt
- 1 teaspoon fresh ground black pepper

Directions:

1. In a bowl, mix dry seasoning, add olive oil, apple cider vinegar.
2. Place the meat in the crockpot, generously coat with seasoning mix.
3. Cover, cook on low for 12 hours.
4. Remove the brisket, place it on a pan. Sear it under the broiler for 2-4 minutes, observe it, so the meat doesn't burn.
5. Wrap it using a foil, then let it rest for 1 hour. Slice and serve.

Nutrition:

Calories: 280

Carbs: 4g

Fat: 20g

Protein: 20g

89. Seriously Delicious Lamb Roast

Preparation time: 15 minutes

Cooking time: 8 hours

Servings: 8

Ingredients:

- medium radishes, scrubbed, washed, and cut in half
- Salt and pepper to taste
- 1 red onion, diced
- 2 garlic cloves, minced
- 1 lamb joint (approximately 4.5 pounds) at room temperature
- 2 Tablespoons olive oil
- 1 teaspoon dry oregano
- 1 teaspoon dry thyme
- 1 sprig fresh rosemary
- cups heated broth, your choice

Directions:

1. Place cut radishes along the bottom of the crockpot. Season. Add onion and garlic.
2. Blend the herbs plus olive oil in a small bowl until it forms to paste.
3. Place the meat on top of the radishes. Knead the paste over the meat.
4. Heat the stock, pour it around the meat.
5. Cover, cook on low for 8 hours. Let it rest for 20 minutes. Slice and serve.

Nutrition:

Calories: 206

Carbs: 4g

Fat: 9g

Protein: 32g

90.   Lamb Provençal

Preparation time: 15 minutes

Cooking time: 8 hours

Servings: 4

Ingredients:

- 2 racks lamb, approximately 2 pounds
- 1 Tablespoon olive oil
- 2 Tablespoons fresh rosemary, chopped
- 1 Tablespoon fresh thyme, chopped
- garlic cloves, minced
- 1 teaspoon dry oregano
- 1 lemon, the zest
- 1 teaspoon minced fresh ginger
- 1 cup (Good) red wine
- Salt and pepper to taste

Directions:

1. Preheat the crockpot on low.
2. In a pan, heat 1 tablespoon olive oil. Brown the meat for 2 minutes per side.
3. Mix remaining **Ingredients:** in a bowl.

4. Place the lamb in the crockpot, pour the remaining seasoning over the meat.

5. Cover, cook on low for 8 hours.

Nutrition:

Calories: 140

Carbs: 3g

Fat: 5g

Protein: 21g

91.   Greek Style Lamb Shanks

Preparation time: 15 minutes

Cooking time: 6 hours

Servings: 8

Ingredients:

- Tablespoons butter
- lamb shanks, approximately 1 pound each
- 2 Tablespoons olive oil
- 8-10 pearl onions
- garlic cloves, minced
- 2 beef tomatoes, cubed
- ¼ cup of green olives
- bay leaves
- 1 sprig fresh rosemary
- 1 teaspoon dry thyme
- 1 teaspoon ground cumin
- 1 cup fresh spinach
- ¾ cup hot water
- ½ cup red wine, Merlot or Cabernet

- Salt and pepper to taste

Directions:

1. Liquify the butter in a pan, then cook the shanks on each side.
2. Remove, then add oil, onions, garlic. Cook for 3-4 minutes. Add tomatoes, olives, spices, then stir well. Put the liquids and return the meat. Boil for 1 minute.
3. Transfer everything to the slow cooker.
4. Cover, cook on medium-high for 6 hours.

Nutrition:

Calories: 250

Carbs: 3g

Fat: 16g

Protein: 22g

92.   Homemade Meatballs and Spaghetti Squash

Preparation time: 15 minutes

Cooking time: 8 hours

Servings: 8

Ingredients:

- 1 medium-sized spaghetti squash, washed, halved
- 1 Tablespoon butter, to grease the crockpot
  - pounds lean ground beef
- 2 garlic cloves
- 1 red onion, chopped

- ½ cup almond flour
- 2 Tablespoons of dry Parmesan cheese
- 1 egg, beaten
- 1 teaspoon ground cumin
- Salt and pepper to taste
- cans diced Italian tomatoes
- 1 small can tomato paste, 28 ounces
- 1 cup hot water
- 1 red onion, chopped
- ¼ cup chopped parsley
- ½ teaspoon each, salt and sugar (optional)
- 1 bay leaf

Directions:

1. Grease the crockpot, place both squash halves open side down in the crockpot.
2. Mix meatball **Ingredients:** in a bowl—form approximately 20 small meatballs.
3. In a pan, heat the olive oil. Fry the meatballs within 2-3 minutes per side. Transfer to the crockpot.
4. In the small bowl, add the tomatoes, tomato paste, oil, water, onion, and parsley, add ½ teaspoon each of salt and sugar. Mix well.
5. Pour the marinara sauce in the crockpot around the squash halves.
6. Cover, cook on low for 8 hours.

Nutrition:

Calories: 235

Carbs: 12g

Fat: 14g

Protein: 15g

93.   Beef and Cabbage Roast

Preparation time: 15 minutes

Cooking time: 8 hours

Servings: 10

Ingredients:

- 1 red onion, quartered
- 2 garlic cloves, minced
- 2-3 stocks celery, diced (approximately 1 cup)
- 4-6 dry pimento berries
- 2 bay leaves
  - pounds beef brisket (two pieces)
- 1 teaspoon chili powder
- 1 teaspoon ground cumin
- 2 cups broth, beef + 2 cups hot water
- Salt and pepper to taste
- 1 medium cabbage (approximately 2.2 pounds), cut in half, then quartered

Directions:

1. Add all Ingredients, except cabbage, to the crockpot in order of the list.
2. Cover, cook on low for 7 hours.
3. Uncover, add the cabbage on top of the stew. Re-cover, cook for 1 additional hour.

Nutrition:

Calories: 150

Carbs: 8g

Fat: 3g

Protein: 22g

Chapter 8. Poultry

94. Aromatic Jalapeno Wings

Preparation time: 10 minutes

Cooking time: 3 hours

Servings: 4

Ingredients:

- 1 jalapeño pepper, diced
- ½ cup of fresh cilantro, diced
- 3 tablespoon of coconut oil
- Juice from 1 lime
- 2 garlic cloves, peeled and minced
- Salt and black pepper ground, to taste
- 2 lbs. chicken wings
- Lime wedges, to serve
- Mayonnaise, to serve

Directions:

1. Start by throwing all the Ingredients into the large bowl and mix well.
2. Cover the wings and marinate them in the refrigerator for 2 hours.
3. Now add the wings along with their marinade into the Crockpot.
4. Cover it and cook for 3 hours on Low Settings.
5. Garnish as desired.
6. Serve warm.

Nutrition:

Calories 246

Total Fat 7.4 g

Saturated Fat 4.6 g

Cholesterol 105 mg

Total Carbs 9.4 g

Sugar 6.5 g

Fiber 2.7 g

Sodium 353 mg

Potassium 529 mg

Protein 37.2 g

95. Barbeque Chicken Wings

Preparation time: 10 minutes

Cooking time: 3 hours

Servings: 4

Ingredients:

- 2 lbs. chicken wings
- 1/2 cup of water
- 1/2 teaspoon of basil, dried
- 3/4 cup of BBQ sauce
- 1/2 cup of lime juice
- 1 teaspoon of red pepper, crushed
- 2 teaspoons of paprika
- 1/2 cup of swerve
- Salt and black pepper- to taste
- A pinch cayenne peppers

Directions:

1. Start by throwing all the Ingredients into the Crockpot and mix them well.
2. Cover it and cook for 3 hours on Low Settings.
3. Garnish as desired.

4. Serve warm.

Nutrition:

Calories 457

Total Fat 19.1 g

Saturated Fat 11 g

Cholesterol 262 mg

Total Carbs 8.9 g

Sugar 1.2 g

Fiber 1.7 g

Sodium 557 mg

Potassium 748 mg

Protein 32.5 g

96.   Saucy Duck

Preparation time: 10 minutes

Cooking time: 6 hours

Servings: 4

Ingredients

- 1 duck, cut into small chunks
- 4 garlic cloves, minced
- 4 tablespoons of swerves
- 2 green onions, roughly diced
- 4 tablespoon of soy sauce
- 4 tablespoon of sherry wine
- 1/4 cup of water
- 1-inch ginger root, sliced

- A pinch salt
- black pepper to taste

Directions:

1. Start by throwing all the Ingredients into the Crockpot and mix them well.
2. Cover it and cook for 6 hours on Low Settings.
3. Garnish as desired.
4. Serve warm.

Nutrition:

Calories 338

Total Fat 3.8 g

Saturated Fat 0.7 g

Cholesterol 22 mg

Total Carbs 8.3 g

Fiber 2.4 g

Sugar 1.2 g

Sodium 620 mg

Potassium 271 mg

Protein 15.4g

97.   Chicken Roux Gumbo

Preparation time: 10 minutes

Cooking time: 6 hours

Servings: 24

Ingredients:

- 1 lb. chicken thighs, cut into halves

- 1 tablespoon of vegetable oil
- 1 lb. smoky sausage, sliced, crispy, and crumbled.
- Salt and black pepper- to taste

Aromatics:

- 1 bell pepper, diced
- 2 quarts' chicken stock
- 15 oz. canned tomatoes, diced
- 1 celery stalk, diced
- salt to taste
- 4 garlic cloves, minced
- 1/2 lbs. okra, sliced
- 1 yellow onion, diced
- a dash tabasco sauce

For the roux:

- 1/2 cup of almond flour
- 1/4 cup of vegetable oil
- 1 teaspoon of Cajun spice

Directions:

1. Start by throwing all the Ingredients except okra and roux Ingredients into the Crockpot.
2. Cover it and cook for 5 hours on Low Settings.
3. Stir in okra and cook for another 1 hour on low heat.
4. Mix all the roux Ingredients and add them to the Crockpot.
5. Stir cook on high heat until the sauce thickens.
6. Garnish as desired.
7. Serve warm.

Nutrition:

Calories 604

Total Fat 30.6 g

Saturated Fat 13.1 g

Cholesterol 131 mg

Total Carbs 1.4g

Fiber 0.2 g

Sugar 20.3 g

Sodium 834 mg

Potassium 512 mg

Protein 54.6 g

98.   Cider-Braised Chicken

Preparation time: 10 minutes

Cooking time: 5 hours

Servings: 2

Ingredients:

- 4 chicken drumsticks

- 2 tablespoon of olive oil

- ½ cup of apple cider vinegar

- 1 tablespoon of balsamic vinegar

- 1 chili pepper, diced

- 1 yellow onion, minced

- Salt and black pepper- to taste

Directions:

1. Start by throwing all the Ingredients into a bowl and mix them well.
2. Marinate this chicken for 2 hours in the refrigerator.

3. Spread the chicken along with its marinade in the Crockpot.

4. Cover it and cook for 5 hours on Low Settings.

5. Garnish as desired.

6. Serve warm.

Nutrition:

Calories 311

Total Fat 25.5 g

Saturated Fat 12.4 g

Cholesterol 69 mg

Total Carbs 1.4 g

Fiber 0.7 g

Sugar 0.3 g

Sodium 58 mg

Potassium 362 mg

Protein 18.4 g

99.   Chunky Chicken Salsa

Preparation time: 10 minutes

Cooking time: 6 hours

Servings: 2

Ingredients

- 1 lb. chicken breast, skinless and boneless
- 1 cup of chunky salsa
- 3/4 teaspoon of cumin
- A pinch oregano
- Salt and black pepper- to taste

Directions:

1. Start by throwing all the Ingredients into the Crockpot and mix them well.
2. Cover it and cook for 6 hours on Low Settings. Garnish as desired.
3. Serve warm.

Nutrition:

Calories 541

Total Fat 34 g

Saturated Fat 8.5 g

Cholesterol 69 mg

Total Carbs 3.4 g

Fiber 1.2 g

Sugar 1 g

Sodium 547 mg

Potassium 467 mg

Protein 20.3 g

100.   Dijon Chicken

Preparation time: 10 minutes

Cooking time: 6 hours

Servings: 4

Ingredients:

- 2 lbs. chicken thighs, skinless and boneless
- 3/4 cup of chicken stock

- 1/4 cup of lemon juice
- 2 tablespoon of extra virgin olive oil
- 3 tablespoon of Dijon mustard
- 2 tablespoons of Italian seasoning
- Salt and black pepper- to taste

Directions:

1. Start by throwing all the Ingredients into the Crockpot and mix them well.
2. Cover it and cook for 6 hours on Low Settings.
3. Garnish as desired.
4. Serve warm.

Nutrition:

Calories 398

Total Fat 13.8 g

Saturated Fat 5.1 g

Cholesterol 200 mg

Total Carbs 3.6 g

Fiber 1 g

Sugar 1.3 g

Sodium 272 mg

Potassium 531 mg

Protein 51.8 g

101. Chicken Thighs with Vegetables

Preparation time: 10 minutes

Cooking time: 6 hours

Servings: 6

Ingredients:

- 6 chicken thighs
- 1 teaspoon of vegetable oil
- 15 oz. canned tomatoes, diced
- 1 yellow onion, diced
- 2 tablespoon of tomato paste
- 1/2 cup of white wine
- 2 cups of chicken stock
- 1 celery stalk, diced
- 1/4 lb. baby carrots, cut into halves
- 1/2 teaspoon of thyme, dried
- Salt and black pepper- to taste

Directions:

1. Start by throwing all the Ingredients into the Crockpot and mix them well.
2. Cover it and cook for 6 hours on Low Settings.
3. Shred the slow-cooked chicken using a fork and return to the pot.
4. Mix well and garnish as desired.
5. Serve warm.

Nutrition:

Calories 372

Total Fat 11.8 g

Saturated Fat 4.4 g

Cholesterol 62 mg

Total Carbs 1.8 g

Fiber 0.6 g

Sugar 27.3 g

Sodium 871 mg

Potassium 288 mg

Protein 34 g

102.   Chicken dipped in tomatillo Sauce

Preparation time: 10 minutes

Cooking time: 6 hours

Servings: 4

Ingredients:

- 1 lb. chicken thighs, skinless and boneless
- 2 tablespoon of extra virgin olive oil
- 1 yellow onion, sliced
- 1 garlic clove, crushed
- 4 oz. canned green chilies, diced
- 1 handful cilantro, diced
- 15 oz. cauliflower rice, already cooked
- 5 oz. tomatoes, diced
- 15 oz. cheddar cheese, grated
- 4 oz. black olives, pitted and diced
- Salt and black pepper- to taste
- 15 oz. canned tomatillos, diced

Directions:

1. Start by throwing all the Ingredients into the Crockpot and mix them well.
2. Cover it and cook for 5 6 hours on Low Settings.
3. Shred the slow-cooked chicken and return to the pot.
4. Mix well and garnish as desired.

5. Serve warm.

Nutrition:

Calories 427

Total Fat 31.1 g

Saturated Fat 4.2 g

Cholesterol 0 mg

Total Carbs 9 g

Sugar 12.4 g

Fiber 19.8 g

Sodium 86 mg

Potassium 100 mg

Protein 23.5 g

103.   Chicken with Lemon Parsley Butter

Preparation time: 10 minutes

Cooking time: 3 hours

Servings: 10

Ingredients:

- 1 (5 – 6lbs) whole roasting chicken, rinsed
- 1 cup of water
- 1/2 teaspoon of kosher salt
- 1/4 teaspoon of black pepper
- 1 whole lemon, sliced
- 4 tablespoons of butter
- 2 tablespoons of fresh parsley, chopped

Directions:

1. Start by seasoning the chicken with all the herbs and spices.
2. Place this chicken in the Crockpot.
3. Cover it and cook for 3 hours on High Settings.
4. Meanwhile, melt butter with lemon slices and parsley in a saucepan.
5. Drizzle the butter over the Crockpot chicken.
6. Serve warm.

Nutrition:

Calories 379

Total Fat 29.7 g

Saturated Fat 18.6 g

Cholesterol 141 mg

Total Carbs 9.7g

Fiber 0.9 g

Sugar 1.3 g

Sodium 193 mg

Potassium 131 mg

Protein 25.2 g

104.   Paprika Chicken

Preparation time: 10 minutes

Cooking time: 8 hours

Servings: 8

Ingredients:

- 1 free-range whole chicken
- 1 tablespoon of olive oil

- 1 tablespoon of dried paprika
- 1 tablespoon of curry powder
- 1 teaspoon of dried turmeric
- 1 teaspoon of salt

Directions:

1. Start by mixing all the spices and oil in a bowl except chicken.
2. Now season the chicken with these spices liberally.
3. Add the chicken and spices to your Crockpot.
4. Cover the lid of the crockpot and cook for 8 hours on Low.
5. Serve warm.

Nutrition:

Calories 313

Total Fat 134g

Saturated Fat 78 g

Cholesterol 861 mg

Total Carbs 6.3 g

Fiber 0.7 g

Sugar 19 g

Sodium 62 mg

Potassium 211 mg

Protein 24.6 g

105.   Rotisserie Chicken

Preparation time: 10 minutes

Cooking time: 8 hours 5 minutes

Servings: 10

Ingredients:

- 1 organic whole chicken
- 1 tablespoon of olive oil
- 1 teaspoon of thyme
- 1 teaspoon of rosemary
- 1 teaspoon of garlic, granulated
- salt and pepper

Directions:

1. Start by seasoning the chicken with all the herbs and spices.
2. Broil this seasoned chicken for 5 minutes in the oven until golden brown.
3. Place this chicken in the Crockpot.
4. Cover it and cook for 8 hours on Low Settings.
5. Serve warm.

Nutrition:

Calories 301

Total Fat 12.2 g

Saturated Fat 2.4 g

Cholesterol 110 mg

Total Carbs 2.5 g

Fiber 0.9 g

Sugar 1.4 g

Sodium 276 mg

Potassium 231 mg

Protein 28.8 g

106. Crockpot Chicken Adobo

Preparation time: 10 minutes

Cooking time: 8 hours

Servings: 6

Ingredients:

- 1/4 cup of apple cider vinegar
- 12 chicken drumsticks
- 1 onion, diced into slices
- 2 tablespoons of olive oil
- 10 cloves garlic, smashed
- 1 cup of gluten-free tamari
- 1/4 cup of diced green onion

Directions:

1. Place the drumsticks in the Crockpot and then add the remaining Ingredients on top.
2. Cover it and cook for 8 hours on Low Settings.
3. Mix gently, then serve warm.

Nutrition:

Calories 249

Total Fat 11.9 g

Saturated Fat 1.7 g

Cholesterol 78 mg

Total Carbs 1.8 g

Fiber 1.1 g

Sugar 0.3 g

Sodium 79 mg

Potassium 131 mg

Protein 25 g

107. Chicken Ginger Curry

Preparation time: 10 minutes

Cooking time: 6 hours

Servings: 4

Ingredients:

- 1 ½ lbs. chicken drumsticks (approx. 5 drumsticks), skin removed
- 1 (13.5 oz.) can coconut milk
- 1 onion, diced
- 4 cloves garlic, minced
- 1-inch knob fresh ginger, minced
- 1 Serrano pepper, minced
- 1 tablespoon of Garam Masala
- ½ teaspoon of cayenne
- ½ teaspoon of paprika
- ½ teaspoon of turmeric
- salt and pepper, adjust to taste

Directions:

1. Start by throwing all the Ingredients into the Crockpot.
2. Cover it and cook for 6 hours on Low Settings.
3. Garnish as desired.
4. Serve warm.

Nutrition:

Calories 248

Total Fat 15.7 g

Saturated Fat 2.7 g

172

Cholesterol 75 mg

Total Carbs 8.4 g

Fiber 0g

Sugar 1.1 g

Sodium 94 mg

Potassium 331 mg

Protein 14.1 g

108.   Thai Chicken Curry

Preparation time: 10 minutes

Cooking time: 2.5 hours

Servings: 2

Ingredients:

- 1 can coconut milk
- 1/2 cup of chicken stock
- 1 lb. boneless, skinless chicken thighs, diced
- 1 2 tablespoons of red curry paste
- 1 tablespoon of coconut aminos
- 1 tablespoon of fish sauce
- 2 3 garlic cloves, minced
- Salt and black pepper-to taste
- red pepper flakes as desired
- 1 bag frozen mixed veggies

Directions:

1. Start by throwing all the Ingredient except vegetables into the Crockpot.
2. Cover it and cook for 2 hours on Low Settings.

3. Remove its lid and thawed veggies.
4. Cover the crockpot again then continue cooking for another 30 minutes on Low settings.
5. Garnish as desired.
6. Serve warm.

Nutrition:

Calories 327

Total Fat 3.5 g

Saturated Fat 0.5 g

Cholesterol 162 mg

Total Carbs 56g

Fiber 0.4 g

Sugar 0.5 g

Sodium 142 mg

Potassium 558 mg

Protein 21.5 g

109. Lemongrass and Coconut Chicken Drumsticks

Preparation time: 10 minutes

Cooking time: 5 hours

Servings: 5

Ingredients:

- 10 drumsticks, skin removed
- 1 thick stalk fresh lemongrass
- 4 cloves garlic, minced
- 1 thumb-size piece of ginger

- 1 cup of coconut milk
- 2 tablespoons of Red Boat fish sauce
- 3 tablespoons of coconut aminos
- 1 teaspoon of five-spice powder
- 1 large onion, sliced
- ¼ cup of fresh scallions, diced
- Kosher salt
- Black pepper

Directions:

1. Start by throwing all the Ingredient into the Crockpot.
2. Cover it and cook for 5 hours on Low Settings.
3. Garnish as desired.
4. Serve warm.

Nutrition:

Calories 372

Total Fat 11.1 g

Saturated Fat 5.8 g

Cholesterol 610 mg

Total Carbs 0.9 g

Fiber 0.2 g

Sugar 0.2 g

Sodium 749 mg

Potassium 488 mg

Protein 63.5 g

110. Green Chile Chicken

Preparation time: 10 minutes

Cooking time: 6 hours

Servings: 6

Ingredients:

- 8 chicken thighs, thawed, boneless and skinless
- 1 (4 oz.) can green chilis
- 2 teaspoons of garlic salt
- optional: add in ½ cup of diced onions

Directions:

1. Start by throwing all the Ingredients into the Crockpot.
2. Cover it and cook for 6 hours on Low Settings.
3. Garnish as desired.
4. Serve warm.

Nutrition:

Calories 248

Total Fat 2.4 g

Saturated Fat 0.1 g

Cholesterol 320 mg

Total Carbs 2.9 g

Fiber 0.7 g

Sugar 0.7 g

Sodium 350 mg

Potassium 255 mg

Protein 44.3 g

111. Garlic Butter Chicken with Cream Cheese Sauce

Preparation time: 10 minutes

Cooking time: 6 hours

Servings: 4

Ingredients:

For the garlic chicken:

- 8 garlic cloves, sliced
- 1.5 teaspoons of salt
- 1 stick of butter
- 2 2.5 lbs. of chicken breasts
- Optional 1 onion, sliced

For the cream cheese sauce:

- 8 oz. of cream cheese
- 1 cup of chicken stock
- salt to taste

Directions:

1. Start by throwing all the Ingredients for garlic chicken into the Crockpot.
2. Cover it and cook for 6 hours on Low Settings.
3. Now stir cook all the Ingredients for cream cheese sauce in a saucepan.
4. Once heated, pour this sauce over the cooked chicken.
5. Garnish as desired.
6. Serve warm.

Nutrition:

Calories 301

Total Fat 12.2 g

Saturated Fat 2.4 g

Cholesterol 110 mg

Total Carbs 1.5 g

Fiber 0.9 g

Sugar 1.4 g

Sodium 276 mg

Potassium 375mg

Protein 28.8 g

112.   Jerk chicken

Preparation time: 10 minutes

Cooking time: 6 hours

Servings: 5

Ingredients:

- 5 drumsticks and 5 wings
- 4 teaspoons of salt
- 4 teaspoons of paprika
- 1 teaspoon of cayenne pepper
- 2 teaspoons of onion powder
- 2 teaspoons of thyme
- 2 teaspoons of white pepper
- 2 teaspoons of garlic powder
- 1 teaspoon of black pepper

Directions:

1. Start by throwing all the Ingredients into the Crockpot.
2. Cover it and cook for 6 hours on Low Settings.
3. Garnish as desired.
4. Serve warm.

Nutrition:

Calories 249

Total Fat 11.9 g

Saturated Fat 1.7 g

Cholesterol 78 mg

Total Carbs 1.8 g

Fiber 1.1 g

Sugar 0.3 g

Sodium 79 mg

Potassium 264 mg

Protein 35 g

113. Spicy Wings with Mint Sauce

Preparation time: 10 minutes

Cooking time: 6 hours

Servings: 6

Ingredients:

- 1 tablespoon of cumin
- 18 chicken wings, cut in half
- 1 tablespoon of turmeric
- 1 tablespoon of coriander
- 1 tablespoon of fresh ginger, finely grated
- 2 tablespoon of olive oil
- 1 tablespoon of paprika
- A pinch of cayenne pepper
- ¼ cup of chicken stock

- Salt and black pepper ground, to taste

Chutney/ Sauce:

- 1 cup of fresh mint leaves
- Juice of ½ lime
- ¾ cup of cilantro
- 1 Serrano pepper
- 1 tablespoon of water
- 1 small ginger piece, peeled and diced
- 1 tablespoon of olive oil
- Salt and black pepper ground, to taste

Directions:

1. Start by throwing all the **Ingredients** for wings into the Crockpot.
2. Cover it and cook for 6 hours on Low Settings.
3. Meanwhile, blend all the mint sauce **Ingredients** in a blender jug.
4. Serve the cooked wings with mint sauce.
5. Garnish as desired.
6. Serve warm.

Nutrition:

Calories 248

Total Fat 15.7 g

Saturated Fat 2.7 g

Cholesterol 75 mg

Total Carbs 0.4 g

Fiber 0g

Sugar 0 g

Sodium 94 mg

Potassium 158 mg

Protein 24.9 g

114.   Cacciatore Olive Chicken

Preparation time: 10 minutes

Cooking time: 6 hours

Servings: 4

Ingredients:

- 28 oz. canned tomatoes and juice, crushed
- 8 chicken drumsticks, bone-in
- 1 cup of chicken stock
- 1 bay leaf
- 1 teaspoon of garlic powder
- 1 yellow onion, diced
- 1 teaspoon of oregano, dried
- salt to taste

Directions:

1. Start by throwing all the **Ingredients** into the Crockpot and mix them well.
2. Cover it and cook for 6 hours on Low Settings.
3. Garnish as desired.
4. Serve warm.

Nutrition:

Calories 297

Total Fat 16.2 g

Saturated Fat 6.5 g

Cholesterol 35 mg

Total Carbs 5.9 g

Sugar 3.3 g

Fiber 1.9 g

Sodium 575 mg

Potassium 155 mg

Protein 8.9 g

115.   Duck and Vegetable Stew

Preparation time: 10 minutes

Cooking time: 5 hours

Servings: 4

Ingredients:

- 1 duck, diced into medium pieces
- 1 tablespoon of wine
- 2 carrots, diced
- 2 cups of water
- 1 cucumber, diced
- 1-inch ginger pieces, diced
- Salt and black pepper- to taste

Directions:

1. Start by throwing all the **Ingredients** except into the Crockpot and mix them well.
2. Cover it and cook for 5 hours on Low Settings.
3. Garnish with cucumber.
4. Serve warm.

Nutrition:

Calories 449

Total Fat 23.4 g

Saturated Fat 1.5 g

Cholesterol 210 mg

Total Carbs 0.4 g

Fiber 1.3 g

Sugar 22g

Sodium 838 mg

Potassium 331 mg

Protein 28.5g

116. Mushroom Cream Goose Curry

Preparation time: 10 minutes

Cooking time: 6.5 hours

Servings: 6

Ingredients:

- 12 oz. canned mushroom cream
- 1 goose breast, fat: trimmed off and cut into pieces
- 1 goose leg, skinless
- 1 yellow onion, diced
- 3 ½ cups of water
- 2 teaspoons of garlic, minced
- 1 goose thigh, skinless
- Salt and black pepper- to taste

Directions:

1. Start by throwing all the **Ingredients** into the Crockpot except cream and mix them well.
2. Cover it and cook for 6 hours on Low Settings.

3. Stir in mushroom cream and cook for another 30 minutes on low heat.
4. Give it a stir and garnish as desired.
5. Serve warm.

Nutrition:

Calories 288

Total Fat 5.7g

Saturated Fat 1.8 g

Cholesterol 60 mg

Total Carbs 2.9 g

Fiber 0.2 g

Sugar 0.1 g

Sodium 554 mg

Potassium 431 mg

Protein 25.6g

117. Colombian Chicken

Preparation time: 10 minutes

Cooking time: 6 hours

Servings: 4

Ingredients:

- 1 chicken, cut into 8 pieces
- 2 bay leaves
- 4 big tomatoes, cut into medium chunks
- 1 yellow onion, sliced
- Salt and black pepper- to taste

Directions:

1. Start by throwing all the **Ingredients** into the Crockpot and mix them well.
2. Cover it and cook for 6 hours on Low Settings.
3. Garnish as desired.
4. Serve warm.

Nutrition:

Calories 481

Total Fat 11.1 g

Saturated Fat 0.1 g

Cholesterol 320 mg

Total Carbs 9.1 g

Fiber 1.7 g

Sugar 3 g

Sodium 203 mg

Potassium 331 mg

Protein 7 g

118.   Chicken Curry

Preparation time: 10 minutes

Cooking time: 6 hours

Servings: 6

Ingredients:

- 3 lb. chicken drumsticks and thighs
- 1 yellow onion, diced
- 2 tablespoons of butter, melted

- 1/2 cup of chicken stock
- 15 oz. canned tomatoes, crushed
- 1/4 cup of lemon juice
- 4 garlic cloves, minced
- 1 lb. spinach, chopped
- 1/2 cup of heavy cream
- 1 tablespoon of ginger, grated
- 1/2 cup of cilantro, diced
- 1 ½ teaspoon of paprika
- 1 tablespoon of cumin, ground
- 1 ½ teaspoon of coriander, ground
- 1 teaspoon of turmeric, ground
- Salt and black pepper- to taste
- A pinch cayenne peppers

Directions:

1. Start by throwing all the **Ingredients** into the Crockpot except lemon juice, cream, and cilantro, then mixes them well.
2. Cover it and cook for 6 hours on Low Settings.
3. Stir in remaining **Ingredients** and cook again for 1 hour on low heat.
4. Garnish as desired.
5. Serve warm.

Nutrition:

Calories 537

Total Fat 19.8 g

Saturated Fat 1.4 g

Cholesterol 10 mg

Total Carbs 5.1 g

Fiber 0.9 g

Sugar 1.4 g

Sodium 719 mg

Potassium 374 mg

Protein 37.6.8 g

119. Chicken Shrimp Curry

Preparation time: 10 minutes

Cooking time: 6 hours

Servings: 6

Ingredients:

- 8 oz. shrimp, peeled and deveined
- 8 oz. sausages, sliced
- 8 oz. chicken breasts, skinless, boneless and diced
- 2 tablespoon of extra virgin olive oil
- 1 teaspoon of creole seasoning
- 3 garlic cloves, minced
- 1 yellow onion, diced
- 1 green bell pepper, diced
- 3 celery stalks, diced
- 1 cup of cauliflower rice
- 1 cup of chicken stock
- 2 cups of canned tomatoes, diced
- 3 tablespoons of parsley, chopped
- 2 teaspoons of thyme, dried
- A pinch cayenne peppers
- 2 teaspoon of Worcestershire sauce
- 1 dash tabasco sauce

Directions:

1. Start by throwing all the **Ingredients** into the Crockpot except shrimp and mix them well.
2. Cover it and cook for 5 hours on Low Settings.
3. Stir in shrimp and cook for another 1 hour on low heat.
4. Garnish as desired.
5. Serve warm.

Nutrition:

Calories 240

Total Fat 22.5 g

Saturated Fat 2.7 g

Cholesterol 15 mg

Total Carbs 7.1 g

Fiber 0g

Sugar 0 g

Sodium 474 mg

Potassium 244 mg

Protein 14.9 g

120. Ground Duck Chili

Preparation time: 10 minutes

Cooking time: 6 hours

Servings: 8

Ingredients:

- 1 yellow onion, cut into half
- 1 garlic heat, top trimmed off

- 2 cloves
- 1 bay leaf
- 6 cups of water
- Salt- to taste

For the duck:

- 1 lb. Duck, ground
- 15 oz. Canned tomatoes and their juices, diced
- 4 oz. Canned green chilies and their juice
- 1 teaspoon of Swerve
- 1 tablespoon of Vegetable oil
- 1 yellow onion, minced
- 2 carrots, diced
- Salt and black pepper- to taste
- Handful cilantro, diced

Directions:

1. Start by throwing all other **Ingredients** into the Crockpot and mix them well.
2. Cover it and cook for 6 hours on Low Settings.
3. Garnish as desired.
4. Serve warm.

Nutrition:

Calories 548

Total Fat 22.9 g

Saturated Fat 9 g

Cholesterol 105 mg

Total Carbs 7.5 g

Sugar 10.9 g

Fiber 6.3 g

Sodium 350 mg

Potassium 433 mg

Protein 40.1 g

Chapter 9.   Vegetables

121.   Butter Green Peas

Preparation time: 10 minutes

Cooking time: 3 hours

Servings: 4

Ingredients:

- 1 cup green peas
- 1 teaspoon minced garlic
- 1 tablespoon butter, softened
- ½ teaspoon cayenne pepper
- 1 tablespoon olive oil
- ¾ teaspoon salt
- 1 teaspoon paprika
- 1 teaspoon garam masala
- ½ cup chicken stock

Directions:

1. In the slow cooker, mix the peas with butter, garlic and the other **Ingredients:**,
2. Close the lid and cook for 3 hours on High.

Nutrition:

calories 121,

fat 6.5,

fiber 3,

carbs 3.4,

protein 0.6

122. Lemon Asparagus

Preparation time: 8 minutes

Cooking time: 5 hours

Servings: 2

Ingredients:

- 8 oz. asparagus

- ½ cup butter

- juice of 1 lemon

- Zest of 1 lemon, grated

- ½ teaspoon turmeric

- 1 teaspoon rosemary, dried

Directions:

1. In your slow cooker, mix the asparagus with butter, lemon juice and the other **Ingredients:** and close the lid.
2. Cook the vegetables on Low for 5 hours. Divide between plates and serve.

Nutrition:

calories 139,

fat 4.6.,

fiber 2.5,

carbs 3.3,

protein 3.5

123. Cheese Asparagus

Preparation time: 10 minutes

Cooking time: 3 hours

Servings: 4

Ingredients:

- 10 oz. asparagus, trimmed
- 4 oz. Cheddar cheese, sliced
- 1/3 cup butter, soft
- 1 teaspoon turmeric powder
- ½ teaspoon salt
- ¼ teaspoon white pepper

Directions:

1. In the slow cooker, mix the asparagus with butter and the other Ingredients, put the lid on and cook for 3 hours on High.

Nutrition:

calories 214,

fat 6.2,

fiber 1.7,

carbs 3.6,

protein 4.2

124. Creamy Broccoli

Preparation time: 15 minutes

Cooking time: 1 hour

Servings: 4

Ingredients:

- ½ cup coconut cream

- 2 cups broccoli florets

- 1 teaspoon mint, dried

- 1 teaspoon garam masala

- 1 teaspoon salt

- 1 tablespoon almonds flakes

- ½ teaspoon turmeric

Directions:

1. In the slow cooker, mix the broccoli with the mint and the other Ingredients.
2. Close the lid and cook vegetables for 1 hour on High.
3. Divide between plates and serve.

Nutrition:

calories 102,

fat 9,

fiber 1.9,

carbs 4.3,

protein 2.5

125.   Curry Cauliflower

Preparation time: 15 minutes

Cooking time: 2.5 hours

Servings: 4

Ingredients:

- 1 ½ cup cauliflower, trimmed and florets separated
- 1 tablespoon curry paste
- ½ cup coconut cream
- 1 teaspoon butter
- ½ teaspoon garam masala
- ¾ cup chives, chopped
- 1 tablespoon rosemary, chopped
- 2 tablespoons Parmesan, grated

Directions:

1. In the slow cooker, mix the cauliflower with the curry paste and the other Ingredients.
2. Cook the cauliflower for 2.5 hours on High.

Nutrition:

calories 146,

fat 4.3,

fiber 1.9,

carbs 5.7,

protein 5.3

126. Garlic Eggplant

Preparation time: 15 minutes

Cooking time: 2 hours

Servings: 4

Ingredients:

- 1-pound eggplant, trimmed and roughly cubed
- 1 tablespoon balsamic vinegar
- 1 garlic clove, diced
- 1 teaspoon tarragon
- 1 teaspoon salt
- 1 tablespoon olive oil
- ½ teaspoon ground paprika
- ¼ cup of water

Directions:

1. In the slow cooker, mix the eggplant with the vinegar, garlic and the other Ingredients, close the lid and cook on High for 2 hours.
2. Divide into bowls and serve.

Nutrition:

calories 132,

fat 2.8,

fiber 4.7,

carbs 8.5,

protein 1.6

127. Coconut Brussels Sprouts

Preparation time: 10 minutes

Cooking time: 4 hours

Servings: 6

Ingredients:

- 2 cups Brussels sprouts, halved
- ½ cup of coconut milk
- 1 teaspoon garlic powder
- 1 teaspoon salt
- ½ teaspoon coriander, ground
- 1 teaspoon dried oregano
- 1 tablespoon balsamic vinegar
- 1 teaspoon butter

Directions:

1. Place Brussels sprouts in the slow cooker.
2. Add the rest of the Ingredients, toss, close the lid and cook the Brussels sprouts for 4 hours on Low.
3. Divide between plates and serve.

Nutrition:

calories 128,

fat 5.6,

fiber 1.7,

carbs 4.4,

protein 3.6

128. Cauliflower Pilaf with Hazelnuts

Preparation time: 15 minutes

Cooking time: 2 hours

Servings: 6

Ingredients:

- 3 cups cauliflower, chopped
- 1 cup chicken stock
- 1 teaspoon ground black pepper
- ½ teaspoon turmeric
- ½ teaspoon ground paprika
- 1 teaspoon salt
- 1 tablespoon dried dill
- 1 tablespoon butter
- 2 tablespoons hazelnuts, chopped

Directions:

1. Put cauliflower in the blender and blend until you get cauliflower rice.
2. Then transfer the cauliflower rice in the slow cooker.
3. Add ground black pepper, turmeric, ground paprika, salt, dried dill, and butter.
4. Mix up the cauliflower rice. Add chicken stock and close the lid.
5. Cook the pilaf for 2 hours on High.
6. Then add chopped hazelnuts and mix the pilaf well.

Nutrition:

calories 48,

fat 3.1,

fiber 1.9,

carbs 4.8,

protein 1.6

129. Cauliflower and Turmeric Mash

Preparation time: 10 minutes

Cooking time: 3 hours

Servings: 3

Ingredients:

- 1 cup cauliflower florets

- 1 teaspoon turmeric powder

- 1 cup of water

- 1 teaspoon salt

- 1 tablespoon butter

- 1 tablespoon coconut cream

- 1 teaspoon coriander, ground

Directions:

1. In the slow cooker, mix the cauliflower with water and salt.
2. Close the lid and cook for 3 hours on High.
3. Then drain water and transfer the cauliflower to a blender.
4. Add the rest of the Ingredients, blend and serve.

Nutrition:

calories 58,

fat 5.2,

fiber 1.2,

carbs 2.7,

protein 1.1

130. Spinach and Olives Mix

Preparation time: 15 minutes

Cooking time: 3.5 hours

Servings: 6

Ingredients:

- 2 cups spinach

- 2 tablespoons chives, chopped

- 5 oz. Cheddar cheese, shredded

- ½ cup heavy cream

- 1 teaspoon ground black pepper

- ½ teaspoon salt

- 1 cup black olives, pitted and halved

- 1 teaspoon sage

- 1 teaspoon sweet paprika

Directions:

1. In the slow cooker, mix the spinach with the chives and the other Ingredients, toss and close the lid.
2. Cook for 3.5 hours on Low and serve.

Nutrition:

calories 189,

fat 6.2,

fiber 0.6,

carbs 3,

protein 3.4

131. Paprika Bok Choy

Preparation time: 15 minutes

Cooking time: 2.5 hours

Servings: 6

Ingredients:

- 1-pound bok choy, torn
- ½ cup of coconut milk
- 1 tablespoon almond butter, softened
- 1 teaspoon ground paprika
- 1 teaspoon turmeric
- ½ teaspoon cayenne pepper

Directions:

1. In the slow cooker, mix the bok choy with the coconut milk and the other Ingredients, toss and close the lid.
2. Cook the meal for 2.5 hours on High.

Nutrition:

calories 128,

fat 3.2,

fiber 3.9,

carbs 4.9,

protein 4.1

132. Zucchini Mix

Preparation time: 10 minutes

Cooking time: 3 hours

Servings: 6

Ingredients:

- 1-pound zucchinis, roughly cubed

- 2 spring onions, chopped

- 1 teaspoon curry paste

- 1 teaspoon basil, dried

- 1 teaspoon salt

- 1 teaspoon ground black pepper

- 1 bay leaf

- ½ cup beef stock

Directions:

1. In the slow cooker, mix the zucchinis with the onion and the other Ingredients.
2. Close the lid and cook on Low for 3 hours.

Nutrition:

calories 34,

fat 1.3,

fiber 3.6,

carbs 4.7,

protein 3.6

133.   Zucchini and Spring Onions

Preparation time: 20 minutes

Cooking time: 2 hours

Servings: 8

Ingredients:

- 1-pound zucchinis, sliced
- 1 teaspoon avocado oil
- 1 teaspoon salt
- 1 teaspoon white pepper
- 2 spring onions, chopped
- 1/3 cup organic almond milk
- 2 tablespoons butter
- ½ teaspoon turmeric powder

Directions:

1. In the slow cooker, mix the zucchinis with the spring onions, oil and the other Ingredients.
2. Close the lid and cook for 2 hours on High.

Nutrition:

calories 82,

fat 5.6,

fiber 2.8,

carbs 5.6,

protein 3.2

134.   Creamy Portobello Mix

Preparation time: 15 minutes

Cooking time: 7 hours

Servings: 4

Ingredients:

- 4 Portobello mushrooms
- ½ cup Monterey Jack cheese, grated
- ½ cup heavy cream
- 1 teaspoon curry powder
- 1 teaspoon basil, dried
- ½ teaspoon salt
- 1 teaspoon olive oil

Directions:

1. In the slow cooker, mix the mushrooms with the cheese and the other Ingredients.
2. Close the lid and cook the meal for 7 hours on Low.

Nutrition:

calories 126,

fat 5.1,

fiber 1.6,

carbs 5.9,

protein 4.4

135.   Eggplant Mash

Preparation time: 10 minutes

Cooking time: 2.5 hours

Servings: 2

Ingredients:

- 7 oz. eggplant, trimmed
- 1 tablespoon butter
- 1 teaspoon basil, dried
- 1 teaspoon chili powder
- ½ teaspoon garlic powder
- 1/3 cup water
- ½ teaspoon salt

Directions:

1. Peel the eggplant and rub with salt.
2. Then put it in the slow cooker and water.
3. Close the lid and cook the eggplant for 2.5 hours on High.
4. Then drain water and mash the eggplant.
5. Add the rest of the Ingredients, whisk and serve.

Nutrition:

calories 206,

fat 6.2,

fiber 3.6,

carbs 7.9,

protein 8.6

136. Cheddar Artichoke

Preparation time: 15 minutes

Cooking time: 3 hours

Servings: 6

Ingredients:

- 1 teaspoon garlic, diced
- 1 tablespoon olive oil
- 1-pound artichoke hearts, chopped
- 3 oz. Cheddar cheese, shredded
- 1 teaspoon curry powder
- 1 cup chicken stock
- 1 teaspoon butter
- 1 teaspoon garam masala

Directions:

1. In the slow cooker, mix the artichokes with garlic, oil and the other Ingredients.
2. Cook the artichoke hearts for 3 hours on High.
3. Divide between plates and serve.

Nutrition:

calories 135,

fat 3.9,

fiber 4.3,

carbs 4.9,

protein 4.3

137. Squash and Zucchinis

Preparation time: 15 minutes

Cooking time: 4 hours

Servings: 6

Ingredients:

- 4 cups spaghetti squash, cubed
- 2 zucchinis, cubed
- ½ cup coconut milk
- ½ teaspoon ground cinnamon
- ¾ teaspoon ground ginger
- 3 tablespoons oregano
- 1 teaspoon butter

Directions:

1. In the slow cooker, mix the squash with the zucchinis, milk and the other Ingredients.
2. Close the lid and cook the vegetables on Low for 4 hours.

Nutrition:

calories 40,

fat 2.2,

fiber 1.8,

carbs 4.3,

protein 1.1

138.   Dill Leeks

Preparation time: 10 minutes

Cooking time: 3 hours

Servings: 3

Ingredients:

- 2 cups leeks, sliced

- 1 cup chicken stock

- 2 tablespoons fresh dill, chopped

- ½ teaspoon turmeric powder

- 1 teaspoon sweet paprika

- 1 tablespoon coconut cream

- 1 teaspoon butter

Directions:

1. In the slow cooker, mix the beets with the stock, dill and the other Ingredients.
2. Cook on Low for 3 hours and serve.

Nutrition:

calories 123,

fat 2.9,

fiber 2.2,

carbs 7.5,

protein 4.3.

139.   Vegetable Lasagna

Preparation time: 20 minutes

Cooking time: 6 hours

Servings: 4

Ingredients:

- 1 eggplant, sliced
- 1 cup kale, chopped
- 3 eggs, beaten
- 2 tablespoons Keto tomato sauce
- ½ teaspoon ground black pepper
- 1 cup Cheddar, grated
- ½ teaspoon chili flakes
- 1 tablespoon tomato sauce
- 1 teaspoon coconut oil
- ½ teaspoon butter

Directions:

1. Place coconut oil in the skillet and melt it.
2. Then add sliced eggplants and roast them for 1 minute from each side.
3. After this, transfer them in the bowl.
4. Toss butter in the skillet.
5. Place 1 beaten egg in the skillet and stir it to get the shape of a pancake.
6. Roast the egg pancake for 1 minute from each side.
7. Repeat the steps with remaining eggs.
8. Separate the eggplants into 2 parts.
9. Place 1 part of eggplants in the slow cooker. You should make the eggplant layer.
10. Then add ½ cup chopped parsley and 1 egg pancake.
11. Sprinkle the egg pancakes with 1/3 cup of Parmesan.

12. Then add remaining eggplants and second egg pancake.

13. Sprinkle it with ½ part of remaining Parmesan and top with the last egg pancake.

14. Then spread it with tomato sauce, kale and sprinkle with chili flakes and ground black pepper.

15. Add tomato sauce and top lasagna with remaining cheese.

16. Close the lid and cook lasagna for 6 hours on Low.

Nutrition:

calories 257,

fat 15.9,

fiber 4.5,

carbs 10.5,

protein 21.5

140. Cauliflower Rice Mix

Preparation time: 15 minutes

Cooking time: 2 hours

Servings: 2

Ingredients:

- 1 cup cauliflower rice

- 1 tablespoon coconut butter

- ¼ teaspoon salt

- ¾ teaspoon turmeric

- 1 teaspoon cayenne pepper

- 1 teaspoon curry powder

- 2 oz. Provolone cheese

- 1 ½ cups chicken stock

Directions:

1. In the slow cooker, mix the cauliflower with the butter and the other **Ingredients:** except the cheese, close the lid and cook on High for 1 hour.

2. Add the cheese, cook on High for 1 more hour, divide between plates and serve.

Nutrition:

calories 131,

fat 4.5,

fiber 2.1,

carbs 6.2,

protein 4.5

141.   Vegetable Cream

Preparation time: 15 minutes

Cooking time: 3 hours

Servings: 4

Ingredients:

- 1 cup heavy cream

- 2 cups broccoli, chopped

- 2 spring onions, chopped

- 1 teaspoon olive oil

- 1 teaspoon salt

- 1 teaspoon ground paprika

- 1 oz. celery stalk, chopped

- 1 cup chicken stock

- 1 tablespoon fresh chives, chopped

- ½ cup mushrooms

Directions:

1. In the slow cooker, mix the broccoli with the onion and the other Ingredients, close the lid and cook on High for 3 hours.
2. Blend using an immersion blender and serve.

Nutrition:

calories 218,

fat 5.6,

fiber 1.9,

carbs 5.6,

protein 4.4

142.   Coconut Okra

Preparation time: 15 minutes

Cooking time: 3 hours

Servings: 6

Ingredients:

- 1-pound okra, trimmed

- 1/3 cup coconut cream

- 1/3 cup butter

- ½ teaspoon salt

- ½ teaspoon turmeric powder

- ¾ teaspoon ground nutmeg

Directions:

1. In the slow cooker, mix the okra with cream, butter and the other Ingredients.
2. Cook okra for 3 hours on High.

Nutrition:

calories 203,

fat 6.7,

fiber 2.5,

carbs 6.2,

protein 3.3

143. Pecan Kale Mix

Preparation time: 15 minutes

Cooking time: 4 hours

Servings: 6

Ingredients:

- 1 cup pecans, chopped
- 2 tablespoons butter, softened
- 1-pound kale, torn
- ¼ teaspoon salt
- 2 tablespoons cilantro, chopped
- 1 teaspoon turmeric

213

- ½ teaspoon onion powder
- 1/2 cup chicken stock

Directions:

1. In the slow cooker, mix the kale with cilantro, pecans and the other **Ingredients:** and close the lid.
2. Cook the mix on Low for 4 hours and serve.

Nutrition:

calories 126,

fat 4.8,

fiber 4.6,

carbs 6,

protein 1.1

144. Mushroom Soup

Preparation time: 6 minutes

Cooking time: 7 hours

Servings: 4

Ingredients:

- 1 cup cremini mushrooms, chopped
- 2 spring onions, chopped
- 1 garlic clove, diced
- 1 tablespoon oregano, chopped
- 1 teaspoon olive oil
- ¾ teaspoon ground black pepper
- 2 cups of water

- 1 cup of coconut milk

Directions:

1. In your slow cooker, mix the mushrooms with spring onions and the other **Ingredients:** and close the lid.
2. Cook the soup for 7 hours on Low.
3. When the soup is cooked, blend with an immersion blender and serve.

Nutrition:

calories 214,

fat 12.5,

fiber 2.2,

carbs 6.7,

protein 2.3

145. Artichoke and Asparagus Mix

Preparation time: 15 minutes

Cooking time: 2 hours

Servings: 4

Ingredients:

- 2 artichokes, trimmed and halved

- 1-pound asparagus, trimmed and roughly chopped

- 2 spring onions, chopped

- 1 tablespoon almond butter

- ½ cup coconut cream

- ½ teaspoon salt

- 1 teaspoon chili pepper

- ¼ jalapeno pepper, minced

- ½ cup chicken stock

Directions:

1. In the slow cooker, mix the artichokes with the asparagus, onion and the other Ingredients, close the lid and cook on Low for 2 hours.

Nutrition:

calories 122,

fat 5.9,

fiber 4.5,

carbs 5.2,

protein 8.4

146. Butter Green Beans

Preparation time: 5 minutes

Cooking time: 4.5 hours

Servings: 6

Ingredients:

- 2 cups green beans, trimmed and halved

- ½ cup butter

- 1 teaspoon salt

Directions:

1. Mix up together snap peas with salt and transfer them in the slow cooker.
2. Add butter and close the lid.

3. Cook the vegetables on Low for 4.5 hours.

Nutrition:

calories 175,

fat 15.5,

fiber 2.5,

carbs 7,

protein 2.8

147. Hot Eggplant Mix

Preparation time: 15 minutes

Cooking time: 2 hours

Servings: 4

Ingredients:

- 1 teaspoon coconut oil, melted
- 3 eggplants, sliced
- 1 teaspoon minced garlic
- 1 red chili pepper, minced
- 1 teaspoon Keto tomato sauce
- 1 tablespoon butter
- 1 teaspoon hot paprika
- 1 teaspoon chives, chopped

Directions:

1. In the slow cooker, mix the eggplants with the coconut oil and the other **Ingredients:** and close the lid.
2. Cook the eggplant mix for 2 hours on Low.

Nutrition:

calories 202,

fat 5.2,

fiber 6.5,

carbs 4.5,

protein 5.1

Chapter 10. Beef

148.   Kalua Pork with Cabbage

Preparation time: 10 minutes

Cooking time: 9 hours

Servings: 12

Ingredients:

- 1 medium cabbage head, chopped
- 1 lbs. pork shoulder butt roast, trimmed
- bacon slices
- 1 tbsp. sea salt

Directions:

1. Place 4 bacon slices into the bottom of the slow cooker.
2. Spread pork roast on top of bacon slices and season with salt.
3. Arrange remaining bacon slices on top of the pork roast layer.
4. Cover slow cooker with lid and cook on low for 8 hours or until meat is tender.
5. Add chopped cabbage. Cover again and cook on low for 1 hour.
6. Remove pork from the slow cooker and shred using a fork.
7. Return shredded pork to the slow cooker and stir well.
8. Serve warm and enjoy.

Nutrition:

Calories 264

Fat 18.4 g

Carbohydrates 4.4 g

Sugar 2.4 g

Protein 20.5 g

Cholesterol 71 mg

149.   Creamy Pork Chops

Preparation time: 10 minutes

Cooking time: 6 hours

Servings: 4

Ingredients:

- boneless pork chops
- ½ cup chicken stock
- 1 oz. dry ranch dressing
- oz. chicken soup
- garlic cloves, minced
- Pepper

Directions:

1. Season pork chops with pepper and place in a slow cooker.
2. In a bowl, mix together chicken soup, ranch dressing, stock, and garlic.
3. Pour chicken soup mixture over top of pork chops.
4. Cover slow cooker with lid and cook on low for 6 hours.
5. Serve hot and enjoy.

Nutrition:

Calories 280

Fat 15.1 g

Carbohydrates 7.4 g

Sugar 1 g

Protein 29.1 g

Cholesterol 64 mg

150.   Beef Taco Filling

Preparation time: 10 minutes

Cooking time: 6 hours

Servings: 12

Ingredients:

- 1 lb. ground beef
- oz. can tomato with green chilies
- 1 envelope taco seasoning

Directions:

Add all **Ingredients:** to the slow cooker and stir well.

1. Cover slow cooker with lid and cook on low for 6 hours.
2. Serve and enjoy.

Nutrition:

Calories 75

Fat 2.4 g

Carbohydrates 0.9 g

Sugar 0.6 g

Protein 11.7 g

Cholesterol 34 mg

151.   Flavorful Steak Fajitas

Preparation time: 10 minutes

Cooking time: 6 hours

Servings: 6

Ingredients:

- 2 lbs. beef, sliced
- 2 tbsp. fajita seasoning
- 20 oz. salsa
- 1 large onion, sliced
- 1 bell pepper, sliced

Directions:

1. Add salsa into the slow cooker.
2. Add remaining **Ingredients:** on top of the salsa and stir to mix.
3. Cover slow cooker with lid and cook on low for 6 hours.
4. Stir well and serve.

Nutrition:

Calories 333

Fat 9.7 g

Carbohydrates 11.9 g

Sugar 5 g

Protein 47.8 g

Cholesterol 135 mg

152.   Garlic Herb Pork

Preparation time: 10 minutes

Cooking time: 8 hours

Servings: 10

Ingredients:

- lbs. pork shoulder roast, boneless and cut into 4 pieces
- ½ tbsp. cumin
- ½ tbsp. fresh oregano
- 2/3 cup grapefruit juice
- garlic cloves
- Pepper and salt

Directions:

1. Add pork roast into the slow cooker. Season with pepper and salt.
2. Add garlic, cumin, oregano, and grapefruit juice into the blender and blend until smooth.

3. Pour blended mixture over pork and stir well.

4. Cover slow cooker with lid and cook on low for 8 hours.

5. Remove pork from the slow cooker and shred using a fork.

6. Return shredded pork into the slow cooker and stir well.

7. Serve warm and enjoy.

Nutrition:

Calories 359

Fat 27.8 g

Carbohydrates 2.1 g

Sugar 1.1 g

Protein 23.2 g

153.   Garlic Thyme Lamb Chops

Preparation time: 10 minutes

Cooking time: 6 hours

Servings: 8

Ingredients:

- lamb chops
- 1 tsp dried oregano
- 2 garlic cloves, minced
- ½ tsp dried thyme
- 1 medium onion, sliced
- Pepper and salt

Directions:

1. Add sliced onion into the slow cooker.
2. Combine together thyme, oregano, pepper, and salt. Rub over lamb chops.
3. Place lamb chops in the slow cooker and top with garlic.
4. Pour ¼ cup water around the lamb chops.
5. Cover slow cooker with lid and cook on low for 6 hours.
6. Serve and enjoy.

Nutrition:

Calories 40

Fat 1.9 g

Carbohydrates 2.3 g

Sugar 0.6 g

Protein 3.4 g

Cholesterol 0 mg

154.   Pork Tenderloin

Preparation time: 10 minutes

Cooking time: 4 hours

Servings: 6

Ingredients:

- 1 ½ lbs. pork tenderloin, trimmed and cut in half lengthwise
- garlic cloves, chopped

- 1 oz enveloppe dry onion soup mix
- ¾ cup red wine
- 1 cup water
- Pepper and salt

Directions:

1. Place pork tenderloin into the slow cooker.
2. Pour red wine and water over pork.
3. Sprinkle dry onion soup mix on top of pork tenderloin.
4. Top with chopped garlic and season with pepper and salt.
5. Cover slow cooker with lid and cook on low for 4 hours.
6. Stir well and serve.

Nutrition:

Calories 196

Fat 4 g

Carbohydrates 3.1 g

Sugar 0.9 g

Protein 29.9 g

Cholesterol 83 mg

155. Smoky Pork with Cabbage

Preparation time: 10 minutes

Cooking time: 8 hours

Servings: 6

Ingredients:

- lbs. pastured pork roast
- 1/3 cup liquid smoke
- 1/2 cabbage head, chopped
- 1 cup water
- 1 tbsp. kosher salt

Directions:

1. Rub pork with kosher salt and place into the slow cooker.
2. Pour liquid smoke over the pork. Add water.
3. Cover slow cooker with lid and cook on low for 7 hours.
4. Remove pork from the slow cooker and add cabbage to the bottom of the slow cooker.
5. Now place pork on top of the cabbage.
6. Cover again and cook for 1 hour more.
7. Shred pork with a fork and serves.

Nutrition:

Calories 484

Fat 21.5 g

Carbohydrates 3.5 g

Sugar 1.9 g

Protein 65.4 g

Cholesterol 195 mg

156.   Simple Roasted Pork Shoulder

Preparation time: 10 minutes

Cooking time: 9 hours

Servings: 8

Ingredients:

- lbs. pork shoulder
- 1 tsp garlic powder
- 1/2 cup water
- 1/2 tsp black pepper
- 1/2 tsp sea salt

Directions:

1. Season pork with garlic powder, pepper, and salt and place in a slow cooker. Add water.
2. Cover slow cooker with lid and cook on high for 1 hour, then turn heat to low and cook for 8 hours.
3. Remove meat from the slow cooker and shred using a fork.
4. Serve and enjoy.

Nutrition:

Calories 664

Fat 48.5 g

Carbohydrates 0.3 g

Sugar 0.1 g

Protein 52.9 g

Cholesterol 204 mg

157. Flavors Pork Chops

Preparation time: 10 minutes

Cooking time: 4 hours

Servings: 4

Ingredients:

- pork chops
- 2 garlic cloves, minced
- 1 cup chicken broth
- 1 tbsp. poultry seasoning
- 1/4 cup olive oil
- Pepper and salt

Directions:

1. In a bowl, whisk together olive oil, poultry seasoning, garlic, broth, pepper, and salt.
2. Pour olive oil mixture into the slow cooker, then place pork chops into the slow cooker.
3. Cover slow cooker with lid and cook on high for 4 hours.
4. Serve and enjoy.

Nutrition:

Calories 386

Fat 32.9 g

Carbohydrates 2.9 g

Sugar 0.7 g

Protein 19.7 g

158.   Beef Stroganoff

Preparation time: 10 minutes

Cooking time: 8 hours

Servings: 2

Ingredients:

- 1/2 lb. beef stew meat
- 1/2 cup sour cream
- o oz. mushrooms, sliced
- oz. mushroom soup
- 1 medium onion, chopped
- Pepper and salt

Directions:

1. Add all **Ingredients:** except sour cream into the slow cooker and mix well.
2. Cover slow cooker with lid and cook on low for 8 hours.
3. Add sour cream and stir well.
4. Serve and enjoy.

Nutrition:

Calories 471

Fat 25.3 g

Carbohydrates 8.6 g

Sugar 3.1 g

Protein 48.9 g

Cholesterol 109 mg

159.   Chili Lime Beef

Preparation time: 10 minutes

Cooking time: 6 hours

Servings: 4

Ingredients:

- 1 lb. beef chuck roast
- 1 tsp chili powder
- 2 cups lemon-lime soda
- 1 fresh lime juice
- 1 garlic clove, crushed
- 1/2 tsp salt

Directions:

1. Place beef chuck roast into the slow cooker.
2. Season roast with garlic, chili powder, and salt.
3. Pour lemon-lime soda over the roast.
4. Cover slow cooker with lid and cook on low for 6 hours. Shred the meat using a fork.
5. Add lime juice over shredded roast and serve.

Nutrition:

Calories 355

Fat 16.8 g

Carbohydrates 14 g

Sugar 11.3 g

Protein 35.5 g

Cholesterol 120 mg

160. Beef in Sauce

Preparation time: 10 minutes

Cooking time: 9 hours

Servings: 4

Ingredients:

- 1-pound beef stew meat, chopped
- 1 teaspoon gram masala
- 1 cup of water
- 1 tablespoon flour
- 1 teaspoon garlic powder
- 1 onion, diced

Directions

1. Whisk flour with water until smooth and pour the liquid into the slow cooker.
2. Add gram masala and beef stew meat.

3. After this, add onion and garlic powder.

4. Close the lid and cook the meat on low for 9 hours.

5. Serve the cooked beef with thick gravy from the slow cooker.

Nutrition :

231 calories,

35g protein,

4.6g carbohydrates,

7.1g fat,

0.7g fiber,

101mg cholesterol,

79mg sodium,

507mg potassium

161.   Beef with Greens

Preparation time: 15 minutes

Cooking time: 8 hours

Servings: 3

Ingredients:

- 1 cup fresh spinach, chopped
- oz. beef stew meat, cubed
- 1 cup Swiss chard, chopped
- 2 cups of water

- 1 teaspoon olive oil
- 1 teaspoon dried rosemary

Directions:

1. Heat olive oil in the skillet.
2. Add beef and roast it for 1 minute per side.
3. Then transfer the meat to the slow cooker.
4. Add Swiss chard, spinach, water, and rosemary.
5. Close the lid and cook the meal on Low for 8 hours.

Nutrition :

177 calories,

26.3g protein,

1.1g carbohydrates,

7g fat,

0.6g fiber,

76mg cholesterol,

95mg sodium,

449mg potassium.

162.   Beef and Scallions Bowl

Preparation time: 10 minutes

Cooking time: 5 hours

Servings: 4

Ingredients:

- 1 teaspoon chili powder
- 2 oz. scallions, chopped
- 1-pound beef stew meat, cubed
- 1 cup corn kernels, frozen
- 1 cup of water
- 2 tablespoons tomato paste
- 1 teaspoon minced garlic

Directions:

1. Mix water with tomato paste and pour the liquid into the slow cooker.
2. Add chili powder, beef, corn kernels, and minced garlic.
3. Close the lid and cook the meal on high for 5 hours.
4. When the meal is cooked, transfer the mixture to the bowls and top with scallions.

Nutrition :

258 calories,

36.4g protein,

0.4g carbohydrates,

7.7g fat,

2g fiber,

101mg cholesterol,

99mg sodium,

697mg potassium.

163.   Beef and Artichokes Bowls

Preparation time: 10 minutes

Cooking time: 7 hours

Servings: 2

Ingredients:

- oz. beef sirloin, chopped
- ½ teaspoon cayenne pepper
- ½ teaspoon white pepper
- artichoke hearts, chopped
- 1 cup of water
- 1 teaspoon salt

Directions:

1. Mix meat with white pepper and cayenne pepper. Transfer it to the slow cooker bowl.
2. Add salt, artichoke hearts, and water.
3. Close the lid and cook the meal on Low for 7 hours.

Nutrition :

313 calories,

36.5g protein,

4.6g carbohydrates,

5.9g fat,

17.8g fiber,

76mg cholesterol,

1527mg sodium,

1559mg potassium.

164.   Mustard Beef

Preparation time: 10 minutes

Cooking time: 8 hours

Servings: 4

Ingredients:

- 1-pound beef sirloin, chopped
- 1 tablespoon capers, drained
- 1 cup of water
- 2 tablespoons mustard
- 1 tablespoon coconut oil

Directions:

1. Mix meat with mustard and leave for 10 minutes to marinate.
2. Then melt the coconut oil in the skillet.
3. Add meat and roast it for 1 minute per side on high heat.
4. After this, transfer the meat to the slow cooker.
5. Add water and capers.
6. Cook the meal on Low for 8 hours.

Nutrition :

267 calories,

35.9g protein,

2.1g carbohydrates,

12.1g fat,

0.9g fiber,

101mg cholesterol,

140mg sodium,

496mg potassium.

165.   Beef Masala

Preparation time: 15 minutes

Cooking time: 9 hours

Servings: 6

Ingredients:

- 1-pound beef sirloin, sliced
- 1 teaspoon gram masala
- 2 tablespoons lemon juice
- 1 teaspoon ground paprika
- ½ cup of coconut milk
- 1 teaspoon dried mint

Directions:

1. In the bowl, mix coconut milk with dried mint, ground paprika, lemon juice, and gram masala.
2. Then add beef sirloin and mix the mixture. Leave it for at least 10 minutes to marinate.
3. Then transfer the mixture to the slow cooker.
4. Cook it on Low for 9 hours.

Nutrition :

283 calories,

35.3g protein,

2.2g carbohydrates,

14.4g fat,

0.9g fiber,

101mg cholesterol,

82mg sodium,

560mg potassium.

166.   Beef Sauté with Endives

Preparation time: 10 minutes

Cooking time: 8 hours

Servings: 4

Ingredients:

- 1-pound beef sirloin, chopped
- oz. endives, roughly chopped
- 1 teaspoon peppercorns
- 1 carrot, diced
- 1 onion, sliced
- 1 cup of water
- ½ cup tomato juice

Directions:

1. Mix beef with onion, carrot, and peppercorns.
2. Place the mixture in the slow cooker.
3. Add water and tomato juice.
4. Then close the lid and cook it on High for 5 hours.
5. After this, add endives and cook the meal for 3 hours on Low.

Nutrition :

238 calories,

35.4g protein,

6.4g carbohydrates,

7.2g fat,

1.9g fiber,

101mg cholesterol,

175mg sodium,

689mg potassium.

167. Sweet Beef

Preparation time: 10 minutes

Cooking time: 5 hours

Servings: 4

Ingredients:

- 1-pound beef roast, sliced
- 1 tablespoon maple syrup
- 2 tablespoons lemon juice
- 1 teaspoon dried oregano
- 1 cup of water

Directions:

1. Mix water with maple syrup, lemon juice, and dried oregano.
2. Then pour the liquid into the slow cooker.
3. Add beef roast and close the lid.
4. Cook the meal on High for 5 hours.

Nutrition :

227 calories,

34.5g protein,

3.8g carbohydrates,

7.2g fat,

0.2g fiber,

101mg cholesterol,

78mg sodium,

483mg potassium.

168.   Thyme Beef

Preparation time: 15 minutes

Cooking time: 5 hours

Servings: 2

Ingredients:

- oz. beef sirloin, chopped
- 1 tablespoon dried thyme
- 1 tablespoon olive oil
- ½ cup of water
- 1 teaspoon salt

Directions:

1. Preheat the skillet well.
2. Then mix beef with dried thyme and olive oil.
3. Put the meat in the hot skillet and roast for 2 minutes per side on high heat.
4. Then transfer the meat to the slow cooker.
5. Add salt and water.
6. Cook the meal on High for 5 hours.

Nutrition :

274 calories,

34.5g protein

0.9g carbohydrates,

14.2g fat,

0.5g fiber

101mg cholesterol,

1240mg sodium,

169. Hot Beef

Preparation time: 15 minutes

Cooking time: 8 hours

Servings: 4

Ingredients:

- 1-pound beef sirloin, chopped
- 2 tablespoons hot sauce
- 1 tablespoon olive oil
- ½ cup of water

Directions:

1. In the shallow bowl, mix hot sauce with olive oil.
2. Then mix beef sirloin with hot sauce mixture and leave for 10 minutes to marinate.
3. Put the marinated beef in the slow cooker.
4. Add water and close the lid.
5. Cook the meal on Low for 8 hours.

Nutrition :

241 calories,

34.4g protein,

0.1g carbohydrates,

10.6g fat,

0g fiber,

101mg cholesterol,

266mg sodium,

467mg potassium.

170. Beef Chops with Sprouts

Preparation time: 10 minutes

Cooking time: 7 hours

Servings: 5

Ingredients:

- 1-pound beef loin
- ½ cup bean sprouts
- 1 cup of water
- 1 tablespoon tomato paste
- 1 teaspoon chili powder
- 1 teaspoon salt

Directions:

1. Cut the beef loin into 5 beef chops and sprinkle the beef chops with chili powder and salt.
2. Then place them in the slow cooker.
3. Add water and tomato paste. Cook the meat on low for 7 hours.
4. Then transfer the cooked beef chops onto the plates, sprinkle with tomato gravy from the slow cooker, and top with bean sprouts.

Nutrition :

175 calories, 2

5.2g protein,

1.6g carbohydrates,

7.8g fat,

0.3g fiber,

64mg cholesterol,

526mg sodium,

386mg potassium.

171.   Beef Ragout with Beans

Preparation time: 10 minutes

Cooking time: 5 hours

Servings: 5

Ingredients:

- 1 tablespoon tomato paste
- 1 cup mug beans, canned
- 1 carrot, grated
- 1-pound beef stew meat, chopped
- 1 teaspoon ground black pepper
- 2 cups of water

Directions:

1. Pour water into the slow cooker.
2. Add meat, ground black pepper, and carrot.
3. Cook the mixture on High for 4 hours.
4. Then add tomato paste and mug beans. Stir the meal and cook it on high for 1 hour more.

Nutrition:

321 calories,

37.7g protein,

28g carbohydrates,

6.2g fat,

7.3g fiber,

81mg cholesterol,

81mg sodium,

959mg potassium.

172.   Braised Beef

Preparation time: 8 minutes

Cooking time: 9 hours

Servings: 2

Ingredients:

- oz. beef tenderloin, chopped
- 1 garlic clove, peeled
- 1 teaspoon peppercorn
- 1 teaspoon salt
- 1 tablespoon dried basil
- 2 cups of water

Directions:

1. Put all **Ingredients:** from the list above in the slow cooker.
2. Gently stir the mixture and close the lid.
3. Cook the beef on low for 9 hours.

Nutrition:

239 calories,

33.1g protein,

1.2g carbohydrates,

10.4g fat,

0.3g fiber,

104mg cholesterol,

1238mg sodium,

431mg potassium.

173.   Coconut Beef

Preparation time: 10 minutes

Cooking time: 8 hours

Servings: 5

Ingredients:

- 1 cup baby spinach, chopped
- 1 cup of coconut milk
- 1-pound beef tenderloin, chopped
- 1 teaspoon avocado oil
- 1 teaspoon dried rosemary
- 1 teaspoon garlic powder

Directions:

1. Roast meat in the avocado oil for 1 minute per side on high heat.
2. Then transfer the meat in the slow cooker.
3. Add garlic powder, dried rosemary, coconut milk, and baby spinach.
4. Close the lid and cook the meal on Low for 8 hours.

Nutrition:

303 calories,

27.6g protein,

3.5g carbohydrates,

19.9g fat,

1.4g fiber,

83mg cholesterol,

66mg sodium,

495mg potassium.

174. Beef Roast

Preparation time: 10 minutes

Cooking time: 6 hours

Servings: 5

Ingredients:

- 1-pound beef chuck roast
- 1 tablespoon ketchup
- 1 tablespoon mayonnaise
- 1 teaspoon chili powder
- 1 teaspoon olive oil
- 1 teaspoon lemon juice
- ½ cup of water

Directions:

1. In the bowl, mix ketchup, mayonnaise, chili powder, olive oil, and lemon juice.
2. Then sprinkle the beef chuck roast with ketchup mixture.
3. Pour the water into the slow cooker.
4. Add beef chuck roast and close the lid.

5. Cook the meat on High for 6 hours.

Nutrition:

354 calories,

23.9g protein,

1.8g carbohydrates,

27.3g fat,

0.2g fiber,

94mg cholesterol,

119mg sodium,

230mg potassium.

175. Lunch Beef

Preparation time: 10 minutes

Cooking time: 8 hours

Servings: 2

Ingredients:

- ½ white onion, sliced
- 1 teaspoon brown sugar
- 1 teaspoon chili powder
- 1 teaspoon hot sauce
- ½ cup okra, chopped
- 1 cup of water

- oz. beef loin, chopped

Directions:

1. Mix the beef loin with hot sauce, chili powder, and brown sugar.
2. Transfer the meat to the slow cooker.
3. Add water, okra, and onion.
4. Cook the meal on Low for 8 hours.

Nutrition:

179 calories,

19.3g protein,

7.8g carbohydrates,

7.4g fat,

1.8g fiber,

53mg cholesterol,

520mg sodium,

146mg potassium.

Chapter 11. Seafood & Fish Recipes

176.   Clam Chowder

Preparation time: 10 minutes

Cooking time: 2 hours

Servings: 4

Ingredients:

- Chopped celery – ½ cup
- Chopped onion – ½ cup
- Chicken broth – 1 cup
- Whole baby clams with juice – 2 cans
- Heavy whipping cream – 1 cup
- Salt – ½ tsp.
- Ground thyme – ½ tsp.

- Pepper – ½ tsp.

Directions:

1. Except for the cream, add everything in the Crock-Pot.
2. Cover and cook on high for 1 hour and 45 minutes.
3. Then add the cream and cook on high for 15 minutes more.
4. Serve.

Nutrition:

Calories: 427

Fat: 33g

Carbs: 5g

Protein: 27g

177.   Creamy Seafood Chowder

Preparation time: 10 minutes

Cooking time: 5 hours

Servings: 6

Ingredients:

- Garlic – 5 cloves, crushed
- Small onion – 1, finely chopped
- Prawns – 1 cup
- Shrimp – 1 cup
- Whitefish – 1 cup
- Full-fat cream – 2 cups
- Dry white wine – 1 cup
- A handful of fresh parsley, finely chopped
- Olive oil – 2 tbsp.

Directions:

1. Drizzle oil into the Crock-Pot.
2. Add the white fish, shrimp, prawns, onion, garlic, cream, wine, salt, and pepper into the pot. Stir to mix.
3. Cover with the lid and cook on low for 5 hours.
4. Sprinkle with fresh parsley and serve.

Nutrition:

Calories: 225

Fat: 9.6g

Carbs: 5.6g

Protein: 21.4g

178.   Salmon Cake

Preparation time: 10 minutes

Cooking time: 4 hours

Servings: 4

Ingredients:

- Eggs – 4, lightly beaten
- Heavy cream – 3 tbsp.
- Baby spinach – 1 cup, roughly chopped
- Smoked salmon strips – 4 ounces, chopped
- A handful of fresh coriander, roughly chopped
- Olive oil – 2 tbsp.
- Salt and pepper to taste

Directions:

1. Drizzle oil into the Crock-Pot.
2. Place the spinach, cream, beaten egg, salmon, salt, and pepper into the pot and mix to combine.
3. Cover with the lid and cook on low for 4 hours.

Nutrition:

Calories: 277

Fat: 20.8g

Carbs: 1.1g

Protein: 22.5g

179.   Lemon-Butter Fish

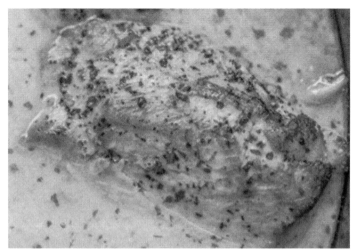

Preparation time: 10 minutes

Cooking time: 5 hours

Servings: 4

Ingredients:

- Fresh white fish – 4 fillets
- Butter - 1 ½ ounce, soft but not melted
- Garlic cloves – 2, crushed
- Lemon – 1 (juice and zest)
- A handful of fresh parsley, finely chopped
- Salt and pepper to taste
- Olive oil – 2 tbsp.

Directions:

1. Combine the butter, garlic, zest of one lemon, and chopped parsley to a bowl.
2. Drizzle oil into the Crock-Pot.
3. Season the fish with salt and pepper and place into the pot.
4. Place a dollop of lemon butter onto each fish fillet and gently spread it out.
5. Cover with the lid and cook on low for 5 hours.

6. Serve each fish fillet with a generous spoonful of melted lemon butter from the bottom of the pot. Drizzle with lemon juice and serve.

Nutrition:

Calories: 202

Fat: 13.4g

Carbs: 1.3g

Protein: 20.3g

180. Salmon with Green Beans

Preparation time: 10 minutes

Cooking time: 3 hours

Servings: 4

Ingredients:

- Salmon fillets – 4, skin on
- Garlic – 4 cloves, crushed
- Broccoli – ½ head, cut into florets
- Frozen green beans – 2 cups

- Olive oil – 3 tbsp., divided
- Salt and pepper to taste
- Water – ¼ cup

Directions:

1. Add the olive oil into the Crock-Pot.
2. Season the salmon with salt and pepper and place into the pot (skin-side down). Add the water.
3. Place garlic, beans, and broccoli on top of the salmon. Season with salt and pepper.
4. Drizzle some more oil over the veggies and fish.
5. Cover with the lid and cook on high for 3 hours.
6. Serve.

Nutrition:

Calories: 278

Fat: 17.8g

Carbs: 8.1g

Protein: 24.5g

181.   Coconut Fish Curry

Preparation time: 10 minutes

Cooking time: 4 hours

Servings: 4

Ingredients:

- Large white fish fillets – 4, cut into chunks
- Garlic cloves – 4, crushed
- Small onion – 1, finely chopped
- Ground turmeric – 1 tsp.
- Yellow curry paste – 2 tbsp.
- Fish stock – 2 cups
- Full-fat coconut milk – 2 cans
- Lime – 1
- Fresh coriander as needed, roughly chopped

- Olive oil – 2 tbsp.
- Salt and pepper to taste

Directions:

1. Add olive oil into the Crock-Pot.
2. Add the coconut milk, stock, fish, curry paste, turmeric, onion, garlic, salt, and pepper to the pot. Stir to combine.
3. Cover with the lid and cook on high for 4 hours.
4. Drizzle with lime juice and fresh coriander and serve.

Nutrition:

Calories: 562

Fat: 49.9g

Carbs: 13g

Protein: 20.6g

182.   Coconut Lime Mussels

Preparation time: 10 minutes

Cooking time: 2 ½ hours

Servings: 4

Ingredients:

- Fresh mussels – 16
- Garlic – 4 cloves
- Full-fat coconut milk – 1 ½ cups
- Red chili – ½, finely chopped
- Lime – 1, juiced
- Fish stock – ½ cup
- A handful of fresh coriander
- Olive oil – 2 tbsp.
- Salt and pepper to taste

Directions:

1. Add olive oil into the Crock-Pot.
2. Add the coconut milk, garlic, chili, fish stock, salt, pepper, and juice of one lime to the pot. Stir to mix.
3. Cover with the lid and cook on high for 2 hours.
4. Remove the lid, place mussels into the liquid, and cover with the lid.
5. Cook until mussels open, about 20 minutes.
6. Serve the mussels with pot sauce. Garnish with fresh coriander.

Nutrition:

Calories: 342

Fat: 30.2g

Carbs: 11.3g

Protein: 10.9g

183.   Calamari, Prawn, and Shrimp Pasta Sauce

Preparation time: 10 minutes

Cooking time: 3 hours

Servings: 4

Ingredients:

- Calamari – 1 cup

- Prawns – 1 cup
- Shrimp – 1 cup
- Garlic – 6 cloves, crushed
- Tomatoes – 4, chopped
- Dried mixed herbs – 1 tsp.
- Balsamic vinegar - 1 tbsp.
- Olive oil – 2 tbsp.
- Salt and pepper to taste
- Water – ½ cup

Directions:

1. Add oil into the Crock-Pot.

2. Add the tomatoes, garlic, shrimp, prawns, calamari, mixed herbs, balsamic vinegar, water, salt, and pepper. Stir to mix.

3. Cover with the lid and cook on high for 3 hours.

4. Serve with zucchini noodles or veggies.

Nutrition:

- Calories: 372

- Fat: 14.6g

- Carbs: 8.5g

- Protein: 55.1g

184.   Sesame Prawns

Preparation time: 10 minutes

Cooking time: 2 hours

Servings: 4

Ingredients:

- Large prawns – 3 cups
- Garlic – 4 cloves, crushed
- Sesame oil – 1 tbsp.
- Toasted sesame seeds – 2 tbsp.
- Red chili – ½, finely chopped
- Fish stock – ½ cup
- Salt and pepper to taste
- Chopped herbs for serving

Directions:

1. Drizzle the sesame oil into the Crock-Pot.

2. Add the garlic, prawns, sesame seeds, chili, and fish stock to the pot. Mix to coat.

3. Cover with the lid and cook on high for 2 hours.

4. Serve hot with fresh herbs and cauliflower rice.

Nutrition:

Calories: 236

Fat: 7.7g

Carbs: 4.3g

Protein: 37.4g

185.   Tuna Steaks

Preparation time: 10 minutes

Cooking time: 3 hours

Servings: 4

Ingredients:

- Tuna steaks – 4
- Garlic – 3 cloves, crushed

- Lemon – 1, sliced into 8 slices
- White wine – ½ cup
- Olive oil – 2 tbsp.
- Salt and pepper to taste

Directions:

1. Reduce the white wine in a pan by simmering until the strong alcohol smell is cooked off.
2. Rub the tuna steaks with olive oil, and season with salt and pepper.
3. Place the tuna steaks into the Crock-Pot.
4. Sprinkle the crushed garlic on top of the tuna steaks.
5. Place 2 lemon slices on top of each tuna steak.
6. Pour the reduced wine into the pot.
7. Cover with the lid and cook on high for 3 hours.
8. Transfer fish on serving plates. Drizzle with pot liquid and serve.

Nutrition:

Calories: 269

Fat: 8.6g

Carbs: 2.9g

Protein: 40.4g

186.   Creamy Smoked Salmon Soup

Preparation time: 10 minutes

Cooking time: 3 hours

Servings: 4

Ingredients:

- Smoked salmon – ½ lb., roughly chopped
- Garlic – 3 cloves, crushed
- Small onion – 1, finely chopped
- Leek – 1, finely chopped
- Heavy cream – 1 ½ cups
- Olive oil – 2 tbsp.
- Salt and pepper to taste
- Fish stock – 1 ½ cups

Directions:

1. Add oil into the Crock-Pot.
2. Add fish stock, leek, salmon, garlic, and onion into the pot.
3. Cover with the lid and cook on low for 2 hours.

4. Add the cream and stir. Cook for 1 hour more.

5. Adjust seasoning and serve.

Nutrition:

Calories: 309

Fat: 26.4g

Carbs: 7g

Protein: 12.3g

187.   Cheese and Prawns

Preparation time: 10 minutes

Cooking time: 1 hour 20 minutes

Servings: 4

Ingredients:

- Shallots – 2, finely chopped
- Apple cider vinegar – ¼ cup
- Butter – 2 tbsp.
- Raw prawns – 4 lbs., peeled, rinsed, patted dry
- Almond meal – 2 tsp.
- Swiss cheese – 1 cup, grated

- Garlic – 2 cloves, peeled, thinly sliced
- Hot pepper sauce – ¼ tsp.
- Salt to taste
- Fresh parsley to serve

Directions:

1. Melt butter in a skillet over medium heat. Then add shallots and sauté for a few minutes until translucent.
2. Add prawns and sauté for 2 minutes. Set aside.
3. Grease the inside of the pot with a little butter.
4. Sprinkle garlic over it and add cheese.
5. In a bowl, mix almond meal, apple cider, and hot sauce. Pour the mixture into the Crock-Pot. Stir.
6. Cover and cook on low for 1 hour.
7. Add the prawn shallot mixture and stir.
8. Cover and cook on low for 10 minutes.
9. Stir again and sprinkle parsley over it.
10. Serve.

Nutrition:

Calories: 238

Fat: 13.5g

Carbs: 9g

Protein: 20g

Chapter 12. Side Dish Recipes

188.   Garlic Carrots Mix

Preparation time: 15 minutes

Cooking time: 4 Hours

Servings: 2

Ingredients:

- 1 pound carrots, sliced
- 2 garlic cloves, minced
- 1 red onion, chopped
- 1 tablespoon olive oil
- ½ cup tomato sauce
- A pinch of salt and black pepper
- ½ teaspoon oregano, dried
- 2 teaspoons lemon zest, grated
- 1 tablespoon lemon juice
- 1 tablespoon chives, chopped

Directions:

1.   In your Crock Pot, mix the carrots with the garlic, onion and then add the other Ingredients, toss, put the lid on and cook on Low for 4 hours.
2.   Divide the mix between plates and serve.

Nutrition:

calories 219,

fat 8,

fiber 4,

carbs 8,

protein 17

189.   Marjoram Rice Mix

Preparation time: 15 minutes

Cooking time: 6 Hours

Servings: 2

Ingredients:

- 1 cup wild rice
- 2 cups chicken stock
- 1 carrot, peeled and grated
- 2 tablespoons marjoram, chopped
- 1 tablespoon olive oil
- A pinch of salt and black pepper
- 1 tablespoon green onions, chopped

Directions:

1.   In your Crock Pot, mix the rice with the stock and after that add the other Ingredients, toss, put the lid on and cook on Low for 6 hours.
2.   Divide between plates and serve.

Nutrition:

calories 200,

fat 2,

fiber 3,

carbs 7,

protein 5

190.   Green Beans and Mushrooms

Preparation time: 15 minutes

Cooking time: 3 Hours

Servings: 4

Ingredients:

- 1 pound fresh green beans, trimmed
- 1 small yellow onion, chopped
- ounces bacon, chopped
- 1 garlic clove, minced
- 1 cup chicken stock
- ounces mushrooms, sliced
- Salt and black pepper to the taste
- A splash of balsamic vinegar

Directions:

1. In your Crock Pot, mix beans with onion, bacon, garlic, stock, mushrooms, salt, pepper and vinegar, stir, cover and cook on Low for 3 hours.
2. Divide between plates and serve as a side dish.

Nutrition:

calories 162,

fat 4,

fiber 5,

carbs 8,

protein 4

191. Beans and Red Peppers

Preparation time: 15 minutes

Cooking time: 2 Hrs.

Servings: 2

Ingredients:

- 2 cups green beans, halved
- 1 red bell pepper, cut into strips
- Salt and black pepper to the taste
- 1 tbsp. olive oil
- 1 and ½ tbsp. honey mustard

Directions:

1. Add green beans; honey mustard, red bell pepper, oil, salt, and black to Crock Pot.
2. Put on the cooker's lid on and set the cooking time to hours on High settings.
3. Serve warm.

Nutrition: Per Serving:

Calories: 50,

Total Fat: 0g,

Fiber: 4g,

Total Carbs: 8g,

Protein: 2g

192. Cabbage and Onion Mix

Preparation time: 15 minutes

Cooking time: 2 Hours

Servings: 2

Ingredients:

- 1 and ½ cups green cabbage, shredded
- 1 cup red cabbage, shredded

- 1 tablespoon olive oil
- 1 red onion, sliced
- 2 spring onions, chopped
- ½ cup tomato paste
- ¼ cup veggie stock
- 2 tomatoes, chopped
- 2 jalapenos, chopped
- 1 tablespoon chili powder
- 1 tablespoon chives, chopped
- A pinch of salt and black pepper

Directions:

1. Grease your Crock Pot with the oil and mix the cabbage with the onion, spring onions and the other **Ingredients:** inside.
2. Toss, put the lid on and cook on High for hours.
3. Divide between plates and serve as a side dish.

Nutrition:

calories 211,

fat 3,

fiber 3,

carbs 6,

protein 8

193.   Cauliflower and Potatoes Mix

Preparation time: 15 minutes

Cooking time: 4 Hours

Servings: 2

Ingredients:

- 1 cup cauliflower florets
- ½ pound sweet potatoes, peeled and cubed
- 1 cup veggie stock
- ½ cup tomato sauce
- 1 tablespoon chives, chopped
- Salt and black pepper to the taste
- 1 teaspoon sweet paprika

Directions:

1. In your Crock Pot, mix the cauliflower with the potatoes, stock and the other Ingredients, toss, put the lid on and cook on High for 4 hours.
2. Divide between plates and serve as a side dish.

Nutrition:

calories 135,

fat 5,

fiber 1,

carbs 7,

protein 3

194. Broccoli Mix

Preparation time: 15 minutes

Cooking time: 2 Hours

Servings: 10

Ingredients:

- cups broccoli florets
- 1 and ½ cups cheddar cheese, shredded

- 10 ounces canned cream of celery soup
- ½ teaspoon Worcestershire sauce
- ¼ cup yellow onion, chopped
- Salt and black pepper to the taste
- 1 cup crackers, crushed
- 2 tablespoons soft butter

Directions:

1. In a bowl, mix broccoli with cream of celery soup, cheese, salt, pepper, onion and Worcestershire sauce, toss and transfer to your Crock Pot.
2. Add butter, toss again, sprinkle crackers, cover and cook on High for hours.
3. Serve as a side dish.

Nutrition:

calories 159,

fat 11,

fiber 1,

carbs 11,

protein 6

195.   Roasted Beets

Preparation time: 15 minutes

Cooking time: 4 Hours

Servings: 5

Ingredients:

- 10 small beets
- teaspoons olive oil

- A pinch of salt and black pepper

Directions:

1. Divide each beet on a tin foil piece, drizzle oil, season them with salt and pepper, rub well, wrap beets, place them in your Crock Pot, cover and cook on High for 4 hours.
2. Unwrap beets, cool them down a bit, peel, and slice and serve them as a side dish.

Nutrition:

calories 100,

fat 2,

fiber 2,

carbs 4,

protein 5

196.   Lemony Pumpkin Wedges

Preparation time: 15 minutes

Cooking time: 6 Hours

Servings: 4

Ingredients:

- 15 oz. pumpkin, peeled and cut into wedges
- 1 tbsp. lemon juice
- 1 tsp. salt
- 1 tsp. honey
- ½ tsp. ground cardamom
- 1 tsp. lime juice

Directions:

1. Add pumpkin, lemon juice, honey, lime juice, cardamom, and salt to the Crock Pot.
2. Put the slow cooker's lid on and set the cooking time to 6 hours on Low settings.
3. Serve fresh.

Nutrition: Per Serving:

Calories: 35,

Total Fat: 0.1g,

Fiber: 1g,

Total Carbs: 8.91g,

Protein: 1g

197. Thai Side Salad

Preparation time: 15 minutes

Cooking time: 3 Hours

Servings: 8

Ingredients:

- 8 ounces yellow summer squash, peeled and roughly chopped
- 12 ounces zucchini, halved and sliced
- 2 cups button mushrooms, quartered
- 1 red sweet potatoes, chopped
- 2 leeks, sliced
- 2 tablespoons veggie stock
- 2 garlic cloves, minced
- 2 tablespoon Thai red curry paste
- 1 tablespoon ginger, grated

- 1/3 cup coconut milk
- ¼ cup basil, chopped

Directions:

1. In your Crock Pot, mix zucchini with summer squash, mushrooms, red pepper, leeks, garlic, stock, curry paste, ginger, coconut milk and basil, toss, cover and cook on Low for 3 hours.
2. Stir your Thai mix one more time, divide between plates and serve as a side dish.

Nutrition:

calories 69,

fat 2,

fiber 2,

carbs 8,

protein 2

198. Eggplants with Mayo Sauce

Preparation time: 15 minutes

Cooking time: 5 Hours

Servings: 8

Ingredients:

- 2 tbsp. minced garlic
- 1 chili pepper, chopped
- 1 sweet pepper, chopped
- 4 tbsp. mayo
- 1 tsp. olive oil
- 1 tsp. salt

- ½ tsp. ground black pepper
- 18 oz. eggplants, peeled and diced
- 2 tbsp. sour cream

Directions:

1. Blend chili pepper, sweet peppers, salt, garlic, and black pepper in a blender until smooth.
2. Add eggplant and this chili mixture to the Crock Pot then toss them well.
3. Now mix mayo with sour cream and spread on top of eggplants.
4. Put the cooker's lid on and set the cooking time to 5 hours on High settings.
5. Serve warm

Nutrition: Per Serving:

Calories: 40,

Total Fat: 1.1g,

Fiber: 3g,

Total Carbs: 7.5g,

Protein: 1g

199.   Summer Squash Medley

Preparation time: 15 minutes

Cooking time: 2 hours

Servings: 4

Ingredients:

- ¼ cup olive oil
- 2 tbsp. basil, chopped
- 2 tbsp. balsamic vinegar

- 2 garlic cloves, minced
- 2 tsp. mustard
- Salt and black pepper to the taste
- 3 summer squash, sliced
- 2 zucchinis, sliced

Directions:

1. Add squash, zucchinis, and all other **Ingredients:** to the Crock Pot.
2. Put the cooker's lid on and set the cooking time to hours on High settings.
3. Serve.

Nutrition: Per Serving:

Calories: 179,

Total Fat: 13g,

Fiber: 2g,

Total Carbs: 10g,

Protein: 4g

200. Garlic Butter Green Beans

Preparation time: 15 minutes

Cooking time: 2 Hours

Servings: 6

Ingredients:

- 22 ounces green beans
- 2 garlic cloves, minced
- ¼ cup butter, soft
- 2 tablespoons parmesan, grated

Directions:

1 In your Crock Pot, mix green beans with garlic, butter and parmesan, toss, cover and cook on High for 2 hours.

2 Divide between plates, sprinkle parmesan all over and serve as a side dish.

Nutrition:

calories 60,

fat 4,

fiber 1,

carbs 3,

protein 1

201.   Green Beans and Red Peppers

Preparation time: 15 minutes

Cooking time: 2 Hours

Servings: 2

Ingredients:

- cups green beans, halved
- 1 red bell pepper, cut into strips
- Salt and black pepper to the taste
- 1 tablespoon olive oil
- 1 and ½ tablespoon honey mustard

Directions:

1.   In your Crock Pot, mix green beans with bell pepper, salt, pepper, oil and honey mustard, toss, cover and cook on High for 2 hours.

2.   Divide between plates and serve as a side dish.

Nutrition:

calories 50,

fat 0,

fiber 4,

carbs 8,

protein 2

202.   Cauliflower Carrot Gratin

Preparation time: 15 minutes

Cooking time: 7 Hours

Servings: 12

Ingredients:

- 16 oz. baby carrots
- 6 tbsp. butter, soft
- 1 cauliflower head, florets separated
- Salt and black pepper to the taste
- 1 yellow onion, chopped
- 1 tsp. mustard powder
- 1 and ½ cups of milk
- 6 oz. cheddar cheese, grated
- ½ cup breadcrumbs

Directions:

1. Add carrots, cauliflower, and rest of the **Ingredients:** to the Crock Pot.
2. Put the cooker's lid on and set the cooking time to 7 hours on Low settings.
3. Serve warm.

Nutrition: Per Serving:

Calories: 182,

Total Fat: 4g,

Fiber: 7g,

Total Carbs: 9g,

Protein: 4g

203.   Minty Peas and Tomatoes

Preparation time: 15 minutes

Cooking time: 3 Hours

Servings: 2

Ingredients:

- 1 pound okra, sliced
- ½ pound tomatoes, cut into wedges
- 1 tablespoon olive oil
- ½ cup veggie stock
- ½ teaspoon chili powder
- Salt and black pepper to the taste
- 1 tablespoon mint, chopped
- 3 green onions, chopped
- 1 tablespoon chives, chopped

Directions:

1. Grease your Crock Pot with the oil, and mix the okra with the tomatoes and the other **Ingredients:** inside.
2. Put the lid on, cook on Low for 3 hours, divide between plates and serve as a side dish.

Nutrition:

calories 70,

fat 1,

fiber 1,

carbs 4,

protein 6

204. Lemon Artichokes

Preparation time: 15 minutes

Cooking time: 3 Hours

Servings: 2

Ingredients:

- 1 cup veggie stock
- 2 medium artichokes, trimmed
- 1 tablespoon lemon juice
- 1 tablespoon lemon zest, grated
- Salt to the taste

Directions:

1. In your Crock Pot, mix the artichokes with the stock and the other Ingredients, and then toss it, put the lid on and cook on Low for 3 hours.
2. Divide artichokes between plates and serve as a side dish.

Nutrition:

calories 100,

fat 2,

fiber 5,

carbs 10,

protein 4

205. Mashed Potatoes

Preparation time: 15 minutes

Cooking time: 6 Hours

Servings: 2

Ingredients:

- 1 pound gold potatoes, peeled and cubed
- 2 garlic cloves, chopped
- 1 cup milk
- 1 cup water
- 2 tablespoons butter
- A pinch of salt and white pepper

Directions:

1. In your Crock Pot, mix the potatoes with the water, salt and pepper, put the lid on and cook on Low for 6 hours.
2. Mash the potatoes; add the rest of the Ingredients, whisk and serve.

Nutrition:

calories 135,

fat 4,

fiber 2,

carbs 10,

protein 4

206. Jalapeno Meal

Preparation time: 15 minutes

Cooking time: 6 Hrs.

Servings: 6

Ingredients:

- 12 oz. jalapeno pepper, cut in half and deseeded
- 2 tbsp. olive oil
- 1 tbsp. balsamic vinegar
- 1 onion, sliced
- 1 garlic clove, sliced
- 1 tsp. ground coriander
- 4 tbsp. water

Directions:

1. Place the jalapeno peppers in the Crock Pot.
2. Top the pepper with olive oil, balsamic vinegar, onion, garlic, coriander, and water.
3. Put the cooker's lid on and set the cooking time to 6 hours on Low settings.
4. Serve warm.

Nutrition: Per Serving:

Calories: 67,

Total Fat: 4.7g,

Fiber: 2g,

Total Carbs: 6.02g,

Protein: 1g

207.   Blueberry Spinach Salad

Preparation time: 15 minutes

Cooking time: 1 Hour

Servings: 3

Ingredients:

- ¼ cup pecans, chopped
- ½ tsp. sugar
- 2 tsp. maple syrup
- 1 tbsp. white vinegar
- 2 tbsp. orange juice
- 1 tbsp. olive oil
- 4 cups spinach
- 2 oranges, peeled and cut into segments
- 1 cup blueberries

Directions:

1. Add pecans, maple syrup, and rest of the **Ingredients:** to the Crock Pot.
2. Put the cooker's lid on and set the cooking time to 1 hour on High settings.
3. Serve warm.

Nutrition: Per Serving:

Calories: 140,

Total Fat: 4g,

Fiber: 3g,

Total Carbs: 10g,

Protein: 3g

208. Dill Mixed Fennel

Preparation time: 15 minutes

Cooking time: 3 Hour

Servings: 7

Ingredients:

- 10 oz. fennel bulbs, diced
- 2 tbsp. olive oil
- 1 tsp. ground black pepper
- 1 tsp. paprika
- 1 tsp. cilantro
- 1 tsp. oregano
- 1 tsp. basil
- 3 tbsp. white wine
- 1 tsp. salt
- 2 garlic cloves
- 1 tsp. dried dill

Directions:

1. Add fennel bulbs and all other **Ingredients:** to the Crock Pot.
2. Put the cooker's lid on and set the cooking time to 3.5 hours on High settings.
3. Serve warm.

Nutrition: Per Serving:

Calories: 53,

Total Fat: 4.1g,

Fiber: 2g,

Total Carbs: 4g,

Protein: 1g

209. Okra and Corn

Preparation time: 15 minutes

Cooking time: 8 Hours

Servings: 4

Ingredients:

- 3 garlic cloves, minced
- 1 small green bell pepper, chopped
- 1 small yellow onion, chopped
- 1 cup water
- 16 ounces okra, sliced
- 2 cups corn
- 1 and ½ teaspoon smoked paprika
- 28 ounces canned tomatoes, crushed
- 1 teaspoon oregano, dried
- 1 teaspoon thyme, dried
- 1 teaspoon marjoram, dried
- A pinch of cayenne pepper
- Salt and black pepper to the taste

Directions:

1. In your Crock Pot, mix garlic with bell pepper, onion, water, okra, corn, paprika, tomatoes, oregano, thyme, marjoram, cayenne, salt and pepper, cover, cook on Low for 8 hours, divide between plates and serve as a side dish.

Nutrition:

calories 182,

fat 3,

fiber 6,

carbs 8,

protein 5

210. Savoy Cabbage Mix

Preparation time: 15 minutes

Cooking time: 2 Hours

Servings: 2

Ingredients:

- 1 pound Savoy cabbage, shredded
- 1 red onion, sliced
- 1 tablespoon olive oil
- ½ cup veggie stock
- A pinch of salt and black pepper
- 1 carrot, grated
- ½ cup tomatoes, cubed
- ½ teaspoon sweet paprika
- ½ inch ginger, grated

Directions:

1. In your Crock Pot, mix the cabbage with the onion, oil and the other Ingredients, toss, put the lid on and cook it on High for two hours.
2. Divide the mix between plates and serve as a side dish.

Nutrition:

calories 100,

fat 3,

fiber 4,

carbs 5,

protein 2

211. Balsamic-glazed Beets

Preparation time: 15 minutes

Cooking time: 2 Hours

Servings: 6

Ingredients:

- 1 lb. beets, sliced
- 5 oz. orange juice
- 3 oz. balsamic vinegar
- 3 tbsp. almonds
- 6 oz. goat cheese
- 1 tsp. minced garlic
- 1 tsp. olive oil

Directions:

1. Toss the beets with balsamic vinegar, orange juice, and olive oil in the insert of Crock Pot.
2. Put the slow cooker's lid on and set the cooking time to 7 hours on Low settings.
3. Toss goat cheese with minced garlic and almonds in a bowl.
4. Spread this cheese garlic mixture over the beets.
5. Put the cooker's lid on and set the cooking time to 10 minutes on High settings.
6. Serve warm.

Nutrition: Per Serving:

Calories: 189,

Total Fat: 11.3g,

Fiber: 2g,

Total Carbs: 12g,

Protein: 10g

212.   Cauliflower Rice and Spinach

Preparation time: 15 minutes

Cooking time: 3 Hours

Servings: 8

Ingredients:

- 2 garlic cloves, minced
- 2 tablespoons butter, melted
- 1 yellow onion, chopped
- ¼ teaspoon thyme, dried
- 3 cups veggie stock
- 20 ounces spinach, chopped
- 6 ounces coconut cream
- Salt and black pepper to the taste
- 2 cups cauliflower rice

Directions:

1. Heat up a pan with the butter over medium heat, add onion, stir and cook for 4 minutes.
2. Add garlic, thyme and stock, stir, cook for 1 minute more and transfer to your Crock Pot.
3. Add spinach, coconut cream, cauliflower rice, salt and pepper, stir a bit, cover and cook on High for hours.
4. Divide between plates and serve as a side dish.

Nutrition:

calories 200,

fat 4,

fibre 4,

carbs 8,

protein 2

213. Cumin Quinoa Pilaf

Preparation time: 15 minutes

Cooking time: 2 Hours

Servings: 2

Ingredients:

- 1 cup quinoa
- 2 teaspoons butter, melted
- Salt and black pepper to the taste
- 1 teaspoon turmeric powder
- 2 cups chicken stock
- 1 teaspoon cumin, ground

Directions:

1. Grease your Crock Pot with the butter, add the quinoa and the other **Ingredients:**, toss, put the lid on and then cook on High for about 2 hours
2. Divide between plates and serve as a side dish.

Nutrition:

calories 152,

fat 3,

fiber 6,

carbs 8,

protein 4

214.   Balsamic Okra Mix

Preparation time: 15 minutes

Cooking time: 2 Hours

Servings: 4

Ingredients:

- 2 cups okra, sliced
- 1 cup cherry tomatoes, halved
- 1 tablespoon olive oil
- ½ teaspoon turmeric powder
- ½ cup canned tomatoes, crushed
- 2 tablespoons balsamic vinegar
- 2 tablespoons basil, chopped
- 1 tablespoon thyme, chopped

Directions:

1. In your Crock Pot, mix the okra with the tomatoes, crushed tomatoes and the other Ingredients, toss, put the lid on and cook on High for 2 hours.
2. Divide between plates and serve as a side dish.

Nutrition:

calories 233,

fat 12,

fiber 4,

carbs 8,

protein 4

215.   Asparagus Mix

Preparation time: 15 minutes

Cooking time: 6 Hours

Servings: 4

Ingredients:

- 10 ounces cream of celery
- 12 ounces asparagus, chopped
- 2 eggs, hard-boiled, peeled and sliced
- 1 cup cheddar cheese, shredded
- 1 teaspoon olive oil

Directions:

1. Grease your Crock Pot with the oil, add cream of celery and cheese to the Crock Pot and stir.
2. Add asparagus and eggs, cover and cook on Low for 6 hours.
3. Divide between plates and serve as a side dish.

Nutrition:

calories 241,

fat 5,

fiber 4,

carbs 5,

protein 12

216.   Tarragon Sweet Potatoes

Preparation time: 15 minutes

Cooking time: 3 Hours

Servings: 4

Ingredients:

- 1 pound sweet potatoes, peeled and cut into wedges

- 1 cup veggie stock
- ½ teaspoon chili powder
- ½ teaspoon cumin, ground
- Salt and black pepper to the taste
- 1 tablespoon olive oil
- 1 tablespoon tarragon, dried
- 2 tablespoons balsamic vinegar

Directions:

1. In your Crock Pot, mix the sweet potatoes with the stock, chili powder and the other Ingredients, toss, put the lid on and cook on High for 3 hours.
2. Divide the mix between plates and serve as a side dish.

Nutrition:

calories 80,

fat 4,

fiber 4,

carbs 8,

protein 4

217.   Classic Veggies Mix

Preparation time: 15 minutes

Cooking time: 3 Hours

Servings: 4

Ingredients:

- 1 and ½ cups red onion, cut into medium chunks
- 1 cup cherry tomatoes, halved
- 2 and ½ cups zucchini, sliced

- 2 cups yellow bell pepper, chopped
- 1 cup mushrooms, sliced
- 2 tablespoons basil, chopped
- 1 tablespoon thyme, chopped
- ½ cup olive oil
- ½ cup balsamic vinegar

Directions:

1. In your Crock Pot, mix onion pieces with tomatoes, zucchini, bell pepper, mushrooms, basil, thyme, oil and vinegar, toss to coat everything, cover and cook on High for 3 hours.
2. Divide between plates and serve as a side dish.

Nutrition:

calories 150,

fat 2,

fiber 2,

carbs 6,

protein 5

218.   Mint Farro Pilaf

Preparation time: 15 minutes

Cooking time: 4 Hours

Servings: 2

Ingredients:

- ½ tablespoon balsamic vinegar
- ½ cup whole grain farro
- A pinch of salt and black pepper
- 1 cup chicken stock

- ½ tablespoon olive oil
- 1 tablespoon green onions, chopped
- 1 tablespoon mint, chopped

Directions:

1. In your Crock Pot, mix the farro with the vinegar and the other Ingredients, toss, put the lid on and cook on Low for 4 hours.
2. Divide between plates and serve.

Nutrition:

calories 162,

fat 3,

fiber 6,

carbs 9,

protein 4

Chapter 13. Dessert Recipes

219. Almond Pie

Preparation time: 15 minutes

Cooking time: 41 minutes

Servings: 8 servings

Ingredients:

- 1 cup almond flour
- ½ cup of coconut milk
- 1 teaspoon vanilla extract
- 2 tablespoons butter, softened
- 1 tablespoon Truvia
- ¼ cup coconut, shredded
- 1 cup water, for cooking

Directions:

1. In the mixing bowl, mix up almond flour, coconut milk, vanilla extract, butter, Truvia, and shredded coconut.
2. When the mixture is smooth, transfer it in the baking pan and flatten.
3. Pour water and insert the steamer rack in the instant pot.
4. Put the baking pan with cake on the rack. Close and seal the lid.
5. Cook the dessert on manual mode (high pressure) for 41 minutes. Allow the natural pressure release for 10 minutes.

Nutrition:

calories 90,

fat 9.1,

fiber 0.9,

carbs 2.6,

protein 1.2

220. Coconut Cupcakes

Preparation time: 15 minutes

Cooking time: 10 minutes

Servings: 6 servings

Ingredients:

- 4 eggs, beaten

- 4 tablespoons coconut milk

- 4 tablespoons coconut flour

- ½ teaspoon vanilla extract

- 2 tablespoons Erythritol

- 1 teaspoon baking powder

- 1 cup water, for cooking

Directions:

1. In the mixing bowl, mix up eggs, coconut milk, coconut flour, vanilla extract, Erythritol, and baking powder.
2. Then pour the batter in the cupcake molds.
3. Pour water and insert the steamer rack in the instant pot.
4. Place the cupcakes on the rack. Close and seal the lid.
5. Cook the cupcakes for 10 minutes on manual mode (high pressure).
6. Then allow the natural pressure release for 5 minutes.

Nutrition:

calories 86,

fat 5.8,

fiber 2.2,

carbs 9.2,

protein 4.6

221. Anise Hot Chocolate

Preparation time: 10 minutes

Cooking time: 2 minutes

Servings: 3 servings

Ingredients:

- 1 tablespoon cocoa powder
- 1 tablespoon Erythritol
- ¼ cup heavy cream
- ½ cup of coconut milk
- ½ teaspoon ground anise

Directions:

1. Put all **Ingredients** in the instant pot bowl. Stir them well until you get a smooth liquid.
2. Close and seal the lid.
3. Cook the hot chocolate on manual (high pressure) for 2 minutes. Then allow the natural pressure release for 5 minutes.

Nutrition:

calories 131,

fat 13.5,

fiber 1.4,

carbs 8.5,

protein 1.5

222. Chocolate Mousse

Preparation time: 10 minutes

Cooking time: 4 minutes

Servings: 1 serving

Ingredients:

- 1 egg yolk

- 1 teaspoon Erythritol

- 1 teaspoon of cocoa powder

- 2 tablespoons coconut milk

- 1 tablespoon cream cheese

- 1 cup water, for cooking

Directions:

1. Pour water and insert the steamer rack in the instant pot.
2. Then whisk the egg yolk with Erythritol.
3. When the mixture turns into lemon color, add coconut milk, cream cheese, and cocoa powder. Whisk the mixture until smooth.
4. Then pour it in the glass jar and place it on the steamer rack.
5. Close and seal the lid.
6. Cook the dessert on manual (high pressure) for 4 minutes. Make a quick pressure release.

Nutrition:

calories 162,

fat 15.4,

fiber 1.2,

carbs 3.5,

protein 4.5

223. Lime Muffins

Preparation time: 10 minutes

Cooking time: 15 minutes

Servings: 6 servings

Ingredients:

- 1 teaspoon lime zest
- 1 tablespoon lemon juice
- 1 teaspoon baking powder
- 1 cup almond flour
- 2 eggs, beaten
- 1 tablespoon swerve
- ¼ cup heavy cream
- 1 cup water, for cooking

Directions:

1. In the mixing bowl, mix up lemon juice, baking powder, almond flour, eggs, swerve, and heavy cream.
2. When the muffin batter is smooth, add lime zest and mix it up.

3. Fill the muffin molds with batter.

4. Then pour water and insert the rack in the instant pot.

5. Place the muffins on the rack. Close and seal the lid.

6. Cook the muffins on manual (high pressure) for 15 minutes.

7. Then allow the natural pressure release.

Nutrition:

calories 153,

fat 12.2,

fiber 2.1,

carbs 5.1,

protein 6

224. Blueberry Muffins

Preparation time: 15 minutes

Cooking time: 14 minutes

Servings: 3 servings

Ingredients:

- ¼ cup blueberries
- ¼ teaspoon baking powder
- 1 teaspoon apple cider vinegar
- teaspoons butter, melted
- 2 eggs, beaten
- 1 cup coconut flour
- 2 tablespoons Erythritol
- 1 cup water, for cooking

Directions:

1. In the mixing bowl, mix up baking powder, apple cider vinegar, butter, eggs, coconut flour, and Erythritol.
2. When the batter is smooth, add blueberries. Stir well.
3. Put the muffin batter in the muffin molds.
4. After this, pour water and insert the steamer rack in the instant pot.
5. Then place the muffins on the rack. Close and seal the lid.
6. Cook the muffins on manual mode (high pressure) for 14 minutes.
7. When the time is finished, allow the natural pressure release for 6 minutes.

Nutrition:

calories 95,

fat 4.5,

fiber 6.1,

carbs 14.6,

protein 3.4

225.   Low Carb Brownie

Preparation time: 15 minutes

Cooking time: 15 minutes

Servings: 8 servings

Ingredients:

- 1 cup coconut flour
- 1 tablespoon cocoa powder
- 1 tablespoon coconut oil
- 1 teaspoon vanilla extract
- 1 teaspoon baking powder

- 1 teaspoon apple cider vinegar
- 1/3 cup butter, melted
- 1 tablespoon Erythritol
- 1 cup water, for cooking

Directions:

1. In the mixing bowl, mix up Erythritol, melted butter, apple cider vinegar, baking powder, vanilla extract, coconut oil, cocoa powder, and coconut flour.
2. Whisk the mixture until smooth and pour it in the baking pan. Flatten the surface of the batter.
3. Pour water and insert the steamer rack in the instant pot.
4. Put the pan with brownie batter on the rack. Close and seal the lid.
5. Cook the brownie on manual mode (high pressure) for 15 minutes.
6. Then allow the natural pressure release for 5 minutes.
7. Cut the cooked brownies into the bars.

Nutrition:

calories 146,

fat 11,

fiber 6.2,

carbs 12.6,

protein 2.2

226.   Pecan Pie

Preparation time: 20 minutes

Cooking time: 25 minutes

Servings: 4 servings

Ingredients:

- 2 tablespoons coconut oil

- 4 tablespoons almond flour

- 4 pecans, chopped

- 1 tablespoon Erythritol

- 2 tablespoons butter

- 1 tablespoon coconut flour

- 1 cup water, for cooking

Directions:

1. Make the pie crust: mix up coconut oil and almond flour in the bowl.
2. Then knead the dough and put it in the baking pan. Flatten the dough in the shape of the pie crust.
3. Then melt Erythritol, butter, and coconut flour.
4. When the mixture is liquid, add chopped pecans.
5. Pour water in the instant pot and insert the steamer rack.
6. Pour the butter-pecan mixture over the pie crust, flatten it and transfer on the steamer rack.
7. Cook the pecan pie on manual mode (high pressure) for 25 minutes.
8. Allow the natural pressure release for 10 minutes and cool the cooked pie well.

Nutrition:

calories 257,

fat 26.1,

fiber 3,

carbs 8.5, protein 3.3

227. Vanilla Flan

Preparation time: 10 minutes

Cooking time: 8 minutes

Servings: 4 servings

Ingredients:

- 4 egg whites
- 4 egg yolks
- ½ cup Erythritol
- 7 oz. heavy cream, whipped
- 3 tablespoons water
- 1 tablespoon butter
- ½ teaspoon vanilla extract
- 1 cup water, for cooking

Directions:

1. In the saucepan, heat up Erythritol and butter. When the mixture is smooth, leave it in a warm place.
2. Meanwhile, mix up water, heavy cream, egg whites, and egg yolks. Whisk the mixture.
3. Pour the Erythritol mixture in the flan ramekins and then add heavy cream mixture over the sweet mixture.
4. Pour water and insert the steamer rack in the instant pot.
5. Place the ramekins with flan on the rack. Close and seal the lid.
6. Cook the dessert on manual (high pressure) for 10 minutes. Then allow the natural pressure release for 10 minutes.
7. Cool the cooked flan for 25 minutes.

Nutrition:

calories 269,

fat 25.8,

fiber 0,

carbs 2.3,

protein 7.4

228. Vanilla Pie

Preparation time: 20 minutes

Cooking time: 35 minutes

Servings: 12 servings

Ingredients:

- 1 cup heavy cream
- eggs, beaten
- 1 teaspoon vanilla extract
- ¼ cup Erythritol
- 1 cup coconut flour
- 1 tablespoon butter, melted
- 1 cup water, for cooking

Directions:

1. In the mixing bowl, mix up coconut flour, Erythritol, vanilla extract, eggs, and heavy cream.
2. Grease the baking pan with melted butter.
3. Pour the coconut mixture in the baking pan.
4. Pour water and insert the steamer rack in the instant pot.
5. Place the pie on the rack. Close and seal the lid.
6. Cook the pie on manual mode (high pressure) for 35 minutes.

7. Allow the natural pressure release for 10 minutes.

Nutrition:

calories 100,

fat 6.8,

fiber 4,

carbs 12.1,

protein 2.9

229. Custard

Preparation time: 10 minutes

Cooking time: 7 minutes

Servings: 4 servings

Ingredients:

- eggs, beaten
- 1 cup heavy cream
- 1 teaspoon vanilla extract
- ¼ teaspoon ground nutmeg
- tablespoons Erythritol
- 1 tablespoon coconut flour
- 1 cup water, for cooking

Directions:

1. Whisk the eggs and Erythritol until smooth.
2. Then add heavy cream, vanilla extract, ground nutmeg, and coconut flour.
3. Whisk the mixture well again.
4. Then pour it in the custard ramekins and cover with foil.
5. Pour water and insert the steamer rack in the instant pot.

6. Place the ramekins with custard on the rack. Close and seal the lid.

7. Cook the meal on manual (high pressure) for 7 minutes. Make a quick pressure release.

Nutrition:

calories 209,

fat 17.9,

fiber 0.8,

carbs 10.3,

protein 9.2

230.   Crème Brule

Preparation time: 25 minutes

Cooking time: 10 minutes

Servings: 2 servings

Ingredients:

- 1 cup heavy cream
- egg yolks
- tablespoons swerve
- 1 cup water, for cooking

Directions:

1. Whisk the egg yolks and swerve together.
2. Then add heavy cream and stir the mixture carefully.
3. Pour the mixture in ramekins and place them on the steamer rack.
4. Pour water in the instant pot. Add steamer rack with ramekins.
5. Close and seal the lid.
6. Cook crème Brule for 10 minutes – High pressure. Allow the natural pressure release for 15 minutes.

Nutrition:

calories 347,

fat 33.5,

fiber 0,

carbs 5.2,

protein 8

231.   Lava Cake

Preparation time: 15 minutes

Cooking time: 18 minutes

Servings: 4 servings

Ingredients:

- 1 teaspoon baking powder
- 1 tablespoon cocoa powder
- 1 cup coconut cream
- 1/3 cup coconut flour
- 1 tablespoon almond flour
- teaspoons Erythritol
- 1 tablespoon butter, melted
- 1 cup water, for cooking

Directions:

1. Whisk together baking powder, cocoa powder, coconut cream, coconut flour, almond flour, Erythritol, and butter.
2. Then pour the chocolate mixture in the baking cups.
3. Pour water in the instant pot. Insert the steamer rack.
4. Place the cups with cake mixture on the rack. Close and seal the lid.

5. Cook the lava cakes on manual (high pressure) for 4 minutes. Allow the natural pressure release for 5 minutes.

Nutrition:

calories 218,

fat 19.2,

fiber 5.9,

carbs 14.2,

protein 3.4

232. Keto Coconut Hot Chocolate

Preparation time: 15 minutes

Cooking time: 4 hours

Servings: 8

Ingredients:

- 5 cups full-fat coconut milk
- 2 cups heavy cream
- 1 tsp vanilla extract
- 1/3 cup cocoa powder
- 3 ounces dark chocolate, roughly chopped
- ½ tsp cinnamon
- Few drops of stevia to taste

Directions:

1. Add the coconut milk, cream, vanilla extract, cocoa powder, chocolate, cinnamon, and stevia to the crockpot and stir to combine.
2. Cook for 4 hours, high, whisking every 45 minutes.
3. Taste the hot chocolate and if you prefer more sweetness, add a few more drops of stevia.

Nutrition:

Calories: 135

Carbs: 5g

Fat: 11g

Protein: 5g

233.   Ambrosia

Preparation time: 15 minutes

Cooking time: 3 hours

Servings: 10

Ingredients:

- 1 cup unsweetened shredded coconut
- ¾ cup slivered almonds
- 3 ounces dark chocolate (high cocoa percentage), roughly chopped
- 1/3 cup pumpkin seeds
- 2 ounces salted butter
- 1 tsp cinnamon
- 2 cups heavy cream
- 2 cups full-fat Greek yogurt
- 1 cup fresh berries – strawberries and raspberries are best

Directions:

1. Place the shredded coconut, slivered almonds, dark chocolate, pumpkin seeds, butter, and cinnamon into the crockpot.
2. Cook for 3 hours, high, stirring every 45 minutes to combine the chocolate and butter as it melts.
3. Remove the mixture from the crockpot, place in a bowl, and leave to cool.
4. In a large bowl, whip the cream until softly whipped.

5. Stir the yogurt through the cream.
6. Slice the strawberries into pieces, then put it to the cream mixture, along with the other berries you are using, fold through.
7. Sprinkle the cooled coconut mixture over the cream mixture.

Nutrition:

Calories: 57

Carbs: 11g

Fat: 1g

Protein: 1g

234.   Dark Chocolate and Peppermint Pots

Preparation time: 15 minutes

Cooking time: 2 hours

Servings: 6

Ingredients:

- 2 ½ cups heavy cream
- 3 ounces dark chocolate, melted in the microwave
- 4 egg yolks, lightly beaten with a fork
- Few drops of stevia
- Few drops of peppermint essence to taste

Directions:

1. Mix the beaten egg yolks, cream, stevia, melted chocolate, and peppermint essence in a medium-sized bowl.
2. Prepare the pots by greasing 6 ramekins with butter.
3. Pour the chocolate mixture into the pots evenly.
4. Put the pots inside the slow cooker and put hot water below halfway up.

5. Cook for 2 hours, high. Take the pots out of the slow cooker and leave to cool and set.
6. Serve with a fresh mint leaf and whipped cream.

Nutrition:

Calories: 125

Carbs: 15g

Fat: 6g

Protein: 1g

235. Creamy Vanilla Custard

Preparation time: 15 minutes

Cooking time: 3 hours

Servings: 8

Ingredients:

- 3 cups full-fat cream
- 4 egg yolks, lightly beaten
- 2 tsp vanilla extract
- Few drops of stevia

Directions:

1. Mix the cream, egg yolks, vanilla extract, and stevia in a medium-sized bowl.
2. Pour the mixture into a heat-proof dish. Place the dish into the slow cooker.
3. Put hot water into the pot, around the dish, halfway up. Set the temperature to high.
4. Cook for 3 hours. Serve hot or cold!

Nutrition:

Calories: 206

Carbs: 30g

Fat: 7g

Protein: 6g

236.   Coconut, Chocolate, and Almond Truffle Bake

Preparation time: 15 minutes

Cooking time: 4 hours

Servings: 8

Ingredients:

- 3 ounces butter, melted
- 3 ounces dark chocolate, melted
- 1 cup ground almonds
- 1 cup desiccated coconut
- 3 tbsp. unsweetened cocoa powder
- 2 tsp vanilla extract
- 1 cup heavy cream
- A few extra squares of dark chocolate, grated
- ¼ cup toasted almonds, chopped

Directions:

1. In a large bowl, mix the melted butter, chocolate, ground almonds, coconut, cocoa powder, and vanilla extract.
2. Roll the mixture into balls. Grease a heat-proof dish.
3. Place the balls into the dish—Cook for 4 hours, low setting.
4. Leave the truffle dish to cool until warm. Mix the cream until soft peak.

5. Spread the cream over the truffle dish and sprinkle the grated chocolate and chopped toasted almonds over the top. Serve immediately!

Nutrition:

Calories: 115

Carbs: 8g

Fat: 10g

Protein: 2g

237.   Peanut Butter, Chocolate, and Pecan Cupcakes

Preparation time: 15 minutes

Cooking time: 4 hours

Servings: 14

Ingredients:

- 14 paper cupcake cases
- 1 cup smooth peanut butter
- 2 ounces butter
- 2 tsp vanilla extract
- 5 ounces dark chocolate
- 2 tbsp. coconut oil
- 2 eggs, lightly beaten
- 1 cup ground almonds
- 1 tsp baking powder
- 1 tsp cinnamon
- 10 pecan nuts, toasted and finely chopped

Directions:

1. Dissolve the dark chocolate plus coconut oil in the microwave, stir to combine, and set aside.

2. Place the peanut butter and butter into a medium-sized bowl, microwave for 30 seconds at a time until the butter has just melted.
3. Mix the peanut butter plus butter until combined and smooth.
4. Stir the vanilla extract into the peanut butter mixture.
5. Mix the ground almonds, eggs, baking powder, and cinnamon in a small bowl.
6. Pour the melted chocolate and coconut oil evenly into the 14 paper cases.
7. Spoon half of the almond/egg mixture evenly into the cases, on top of the chocolate and press down slightly.
8. Spoon the peanut butter mixture into the cases, on top of the almond/egg mixture.
9. Spoon the remaining almond/egg mixture into the cases.
10. Put the pecans on top of each cupcake.
11. Put the filled cases into the slow cooker—Cook for 4 hours, high setting.

Nutrition:

Calories: 145

Carbs: 20g

Fat: 3g

Protein: 4g

238.   Vanilla and Strawberry Cheesecake

Preparation time: 15 minutes

Cooking time: 6 hours

Servings: 8

Ingredients: Base:

- 2 ounces butter, melted

- 1 cup ground hazelnuts
- ½ cup desiccated coconut
- 2 tsp vanilla extract
- 1 tsp cinnamon

Filling:

- 2 cups cream cheese
- 2 eggs, lightly beaten
- 1 cup sour cream
- 2 tsp vanilla extract
- 8 large strawberries, chopped

Directions:

1. Mix the melted butter, hazelnuts, coconut, vanilla, and cinnamon in a medium-sized bowl.
2. Press the base into a greased heat-proof dish.
3. Mix the cream cheese, eggs, sour cream, and vanilla extract, beat with electric egg beaters in a large bowl until thick and combined.
4. Fold the strawberries through the cream cheese mixture.
5. Put the cream cheese batter into the dish, on top of the base, spread out until smooth.
6. Put it in the slow cooker and put hot water around the dish until halfway up.
7. Cook for 6 hours, low setting until just set but slightly wobbly.
8. Chill before serving.

Nutrition:

Calories: 156

Carbs: 4g

Fat: 7g

Protein: 15g

239.   Coffee Creams with Toasted Seed Crumble Topping

Preparation time: 15 minutes

Cooking time: 4 hours

Servings: 6

Ingredients:

- 2 cups heavy cream
- 3 egg yolks, lightly beaten
- 1 tsp vanilla extract
- 3 tbsp. strong espresso coffee (or 3tsp instant coffee dissolved in 3tbsp boiling water)
- ½ cup mixed seeds – sesame seeds, pumpkin seeds, chia seeds, sunflower seeds,
- 1 tsp cinnamon
- 1 tbsp. coconut oil

Directions:

1. Heat-up the coconut oil in a small frypan until melted.
2. Add the mixed seeds, cinnamon, and a pinch of salt, toss in the oil and heat until toasted and golden, place into a small bowl and set aside.
3. Mix the cream, egg yolks, vanilla, and coffee in a medium-sized bowl.
4. Pour the cream/coffee mixture into the ramekins.
5. Place the ramekins into the slow cooker. Put hot water inside until halfway.
6. Cook on low setting for 4 hours.
7. Remove, then leave to cool slightly on the bench.
8. Sprinkle the seed mixture over the top of each custard before serving.

Nutrition:

Calories: 35

Carbs: 4g

Fat: 2g

Protein: 1g

240.   Lemon Cheesecake

Preparation time: 15 minutes

Cooking time: 6 hours

Servings: 10

Ingredients:

- 2 ounces butter, melted
- 1 cup pecans, finely ground in the food processor
- 1 tsp cinnamon
- 2 cups cream cheese
- 1 cup sour cream
- 2 eggs, lightly beaten
- 1 lemon
- Few drops of stevia
- 1 cup heavy cream

Directions:

1. Mix the melted butter, ground pecans, and cinnamon until it forms a wet, sand-like texture.
2. Press the butter/pecan mixture into a greased, heat-proof dish and set aside.
3. Place the cream cheese, eggs, sour cream, stevia, zest, and juice of one lemon into a large bowl, beat with electric egg beaters until combined and smooth.

4. Put the cream cheese batter into the dish, on top of the base.
5. Place the dish inside the slow cooker, then put warm water in halfway up.
6. Cook within 6 hours, low setting.
7. Set the cheesecake on the bench to cool and set.
8. Whip the cream until soft peak, and spread over the cheesecake before serving.

Nutrition:

Calories: 271

Carbs: 33g

Fat: 15g

Protein: 2g

241.   Macadamia Fudge Truffles

Preparation time: 15 minutes

Cooking time: 4 hours

Servings: 25

Ingredients:

- 1 cup roasted macadamia nuts, finely chopped
- ½ cup ground almonds
- ounces butter, melted
- ounces dark chocolate, melted
- 1 tsp vanilla extract
- 1 egg, lightly beaten

Directions:

1. Place the macadamia nuts, almonds, melted butter, melted chocolate, vanilla, and egg into a large bowl, stir until combined.

2. Grease the bottom of the crockpot by rubbing with butter. Place the mixture into the crockpot and press down.

3. Set to cook low setting within 4 hours.

4. Allow the batter to cool until just warm. Take a teaspoon, scoop the mixture out, and roll into balls.

5. Refrigerate to harden slightly. Store the truffle balls in the fridge.

Nutrition:

Calories: 150

Carbs: 19g

Fat: 6g

Protein: 6g

242.   Chocolate Covered Bacon Cupcakes

Preparation time: 15 minutes

Cooking time: 3 hours

Servings: 10

Ingredients:

- 10 paper cupcake cases
- 5 slices streaky bacon, cut into small pieces, fried in a pan until crispy
- 5 ounces dark chocolate, melted
- 1 cup ground hazelnuts
- 1 tsp baking powder
- 2 eggs, lightly beaten
- ½ cup full-fat Greek yogurt
- 1 tsp vanilla extract

Directions:

1. Mix the fried bacon pieces and melted chocolate in a bowl, set aside.
2. Mix the ground hazelnuts, baking powder, eggs, yogurt, vanilla, and a pinch of salt in a medium-sized bowl.
3. Spoon the hazelnut mixture into the cupcake cases.
4. Spoon the chocolate and bacon mixture on top of the hazelnut mixture.
5. Place the cupcake cases into the crockpot. Cook for 3 hours, high setting.
6. Remove the cupcakes from the pot and leave to cool on the bench before storing serving. Serve with whipped cream!

Nutrition:

Calories: 185

Carbs: 27g

Fat: 8g

Protein: 4g

243.   Sugar-Free Chocolate Molten Lava Cake

Preparation time: 15 minutes

Cooking time: 3 hours

Servings: 3

Ingredients:

- 1/2 cup hot water
- 1-ounce chocolate chips, sugar-free
- 1/4 teaspoon vanilla liquid stevia
- 1/4 teaspoon vanilla extract
- 1 egg yolk
- 1 whole egg

- 2 tablespoons butter melted, cooled
- 1/4 teaspoon baking powder
- 1/8 teaspoon salt
- 3 ¾ teaspoons cocoa powder, unsweetened
- 2 tablespoons almond flour
- 6 tablespoons Swerve sweetener divided

Directions:

1. Grease the slow cooker, mix the flour, baking powder, 2 tablespoons cocoa powder, almond flour, and 4 tablespoons of Swerve in a bowl.
2. In a separate bowl, stir in eggs with melted butter, liquid stevia, vanilla extract, egg yolks, and eggs.
3. Mix the wet fixing to the dry ones and combine to incorporate fully. Pour the mixture into the slow cooker.
4. Top the mixture with chocolate chips.
5. Mix the remaining swerve with cocoa powder and hot water in a separate bowl, and pour this mixture over chocolate chips.
6. Cook on low within 3 hours. Once done, let cool and then serve.

Nutrition:

Calories 157

Fat 13g

Carbs 10.5g

Protein 3.9g

244.   Blueberry Lemon Custard Cake

Preparation time: 15 minutes

Cooking time: 3 hours

Servings: 3

Ingredients:

- 2 tablespoons fresh blueberries
- 1/2 cup light cream
- 1/8 teaspoon salt
- 2 tablespoons Swerve sweetener
- 1/4 teaspoon lemon liquid stevia
- 1 1/3 tablespoon lemon juice
- 1/2 teaspoon lemon zest
- 2 tablespoons coconut flour
- 1 ½ egg separated

Directions:

1. Put egg whites into a stand mixture and whip to achieve stiff peaks consistency.
2. Set the egg whites aside, whisk the yolks and the other **Ingredients:** apart from the blueberries.
3. Mix the egg whites into the batter to thoroughly combine, and then grease the slow cooker.
4. Put the batter into it, then top with the blueberries—Cook within 3 hours, low.
5. Let cool when not covered for 1 hour, then keep it chilled for at least 2 hours or overnight.
6. Serve the cake topped with unsweetened cream if you like.

Nutrition:

Calories 140

Fat 9.2g

Carbs 7.3g

Protein 3.9g

245. Slow-Cooked Pumpkin Custard

Preparation time: 15 minutes

Cooking time: 2 hours & 45 minutes

Servings: 3

Ingredients:

- 2 large eggs
- 2 tablespoons butter or coconut oil
- Dash sea salt
- 1/2 teaspoon pumpkin pie spice
- 1/4 cup superfine almond flour
- 1/2 teaspoon vanilla extract
- 1/2 cup pumpkin puree
- 1/4 cup granulated stevia

Directions:

1. Grease a crockpot with butter or coconut oil and set aside. With a mixer, break the eggs into a mixing bowl, and blend until incorporated and thickened.
2. Gently beat in the stevia, then add in vanilla extract and pumpkin puree. Then blend in pumpkin pie spice, salt, and almond flour.
3. Once almost incorporated, stream in coconut oil, ghee, and melted butter. Mix until smooth, then move the mixture into a crockpot.
4. Put a paper towel over the slow cooker to help absorb condensed moisture and prevent it from dripping on your pumpkin custard. Then cover with a lid.
5. Now cook on low for 2 hours to 2 hours 45 minutes, and check the content after two hours elapse.
6. Serve the custard with whipped cream sweetened with a little stevia and a sprinkle of nutmeg if you like.

246.   Almond Flour Mocha Fudge Cake

Preparation time: 15 minutes

Cooking time: 4 hours

Servings: 3

Ingredients:

- 1/8 teaspoon Celtic sea salt
- 1/3 teaspoon vanilla or chocolate extract
- 3 tablespoons hot coffee
- 1/3 teaspoon baking soda
- 6 tablespoons blanched almond flour
- 3 tablespoons sour cream
- 3/4 oz. unsweetened chocolate, melted
- 1 egg
- 1 tablespoon butter or coconut oil
- 6 tablespoons Swerve

Directions:

1. Grease the crockpot with oil. Then beat coconut oil and natural sweetener in a bowl until fully incorporated.
2. Beat in eggs, cream and chocolate. In a bowl, sift baking soda and almond flour and add in the chocolate mixture.
3. Then beat in coffee, salt, and vanilla until well incorporated. Once done, pour the batter into the cooking pot of the slow cooker.
4. Cook on low for 2 to 4 hours or until a toothpick inserted in the cake comes out clean.

Nutrition:

Calories 200

Carbs 5.8

Protein 6g

Fat 18g

247. Slow Cooker Bread Pudding

Preparation time: 15 minutes

Cooking time: 5 hours

Servings: 4

Ingredients:

- 1 tablespoons raisin
- 1/2 teaspoon cinnamon
- 1 1/2 teaspoon vanilla extract
- 1/4 cup swerve
- 1 egg white
- 1 whole egg
- 1 1/2 cups almond milk
- 4 slices of pumpkin bread

Directions:

1. Slice the pumpkin bread into pieces. Then mix all the rest of the fixing in the slow cooker.
2. Cook within 4 to 5 hours, then serve.

Nutrition:

Calories 182

Fat 2g

Carbs 11g

Protein 8g

248. Tiramisu Bread Pudding

Preparation time: 15 minutes

Cooking time: 2 hours

Servings: 4

Ingredients:

- 3/4 teaspoons unsweetened cocoa
- 1/3 teaspoon vanilla extract
- 2 tablespoons mascarpone cheese
- Cooking spray
- 3 1/4 cups Keto bread
- 1 large egg, lightly beaten
  o ounces of almond milk, divided
- 3/4 tablespoons Kahlua (coffee-flavored liqueur)
- 1 3/4 teaspoons instant espresso granules
- 2 tablespoons coconut sugar
- 1.6-ounce water

Directions:

1. Mix the water, coconut sugar, plus instant espresso granules in a saucepan.
2. Boil while occasionally stirring for 1 minute, remove, then mix in the Kahlua liqueur.
3. Whisk the eggs, then the almond milk in a large bowl. Mix in the espresso mixture into it.
4. Put the Keto friendly bread into a greased casserole. Cook it inside the slow cooker within 2 hours, low.
5. Mix vanilla, mascarpone cheese plus the remaining almond milk in a bowl.
6. Garnish with cocoa and serve.

Nutrition:

Calories 199

Fat 9g

Protein 6.7g

Carbs 9g

249. Crock Pot Sugar-Free Dairy-Free Fudge

Preparation time: 15 minutes

Cooking time: 2 hours

Servings: 3

Ingredients:

- A dash of salt
- Dash of pure vanilla extract
- ½ tablespoon coconut milk
- 4 tablespoons sugar-free chocolate chips
- 1/4 teaspoons vanilla liquid stevia

Directions:

1. Mix in coconut milk, stevia, vanilla, chocolate chips plus salt in a slow cooker.
2. Cook within 2 hours, then let it sit within 30 minutes.
3. Mix in within 5 minutes. Put the batter in a casserole dish with parchment paper.
4. Chill, then serve.

Nutrition:

Calories 65

Fat 5g

Carbs 2g

Protein 1g

250. Poppy Seed-Lemon Bread

Preparation time: 15 minutes

Cooking time: 2 hours

Servings: 3

Ingredients:

- 1/2 cups almond flour
- 1/4 tbsp. baking powder
- 1 tbsp. poppy seeds
- 1 egg
- 1/4 cup coconut sugar
- 1/8 tsp salt
- 2 tbsp. vegetable oil
- 3 tbsp. tofu (puree)
- 1/4 cup almond milk
- 3/4 cup plain Greek-style yogurt
- 1/4 cup lemon juice
- 3/4 tsp shredded lemon peel
- 1/4 tsp vanilla

Directions:

1. Grease the slow cooker using a non-stick cooking spray.
2. Mix the poppy seeds, flour, salt, and baking powder in a bowl, then put it aside.
3. Mix the tofu puree, sugar, oil, milk, yogurt, lemon juice, lemon peel, and vanilla in a medium bowl.
4. Put the sugar batter to the flour batter, then mix.
5. Transfer it in the slow cooker, then cook on high for 1 and 30 minutes to 2 hours, or until set.
6. Leave for 10-15 minutes to cool. then serve.

Nutrition:

Calories 295.6

Fat 24.3g

Carbs 17.9g

Protein 6.0g

Conclusion

Now you can cook healthier meals for yourself, your family, and your friends that will get your metabolism running at the peak of perfection and will help you feel healthy, lose weight, and maintain a healthy balanced diet. A new diet isn't so bad when you have so many options from which to choose. You may miss your carbs, but with all these tasty recipes at your fingertips, you'll find them easily replaced with new favorites.

You will marvel at how much energy you have after sweating though the first week or so of almost no carbs. It can be a challenge, but you can do it! Pretty soon you won't miss those things that bogged down your metabolism as well as your thinking and made you tired and cranky. You will feel like you can rule the world and do anything, once your body is purged of heavy carbs and you start eating things that rejuvenate your body. It is worth the few detox symptoms when you actually start enjoying the food you are eating.

A Keto diet isn't one that you can keep going on and off. It will take your body some time to get adjusted and for ketosis to set in. This process could take anywhere between two to seven days. It is dependent on the level of activity, your body type and the food that you are eating.

There are various mobile applications that you can make use of for tracking your carbohydrate intake. There are paid and free applications as well. These apps will help you in keeping a track of your total carbohydrate and fiber intake. However, you won't be able to track your net carb intake. MyFitnessPal is one of the popular apps. You just need to open the app store on your smartphone, and you can select an app from the various apps that are available.

The amount of weight that you will lose will depend on you. If you add exercise to your daily routine, then the weight loss will be greater. If you cut down on foods that stall weight loss, then this will speed up the process. For instance, completely cutting out things like artificial sweeteners, dairy and wheat products and other related products will definitely help in speeding up your weight loss. During the first two weeks of the Keto diet, you will end up losing all the excess water weight. Ketosis has a diuretic effect on the body, and you might end up losing a couple of pounds within the first few days of this diet. After this, your body will adapt itself to burning fats for generating energy, instead of carbs.

You now have everything you need to break free from a dependence on highly processed foods, with all their dangerous additives that your body interprets as toxins. Today, when you want a sandwich for lunch, you'll roll the meat in Swiss cheese or a lettuce leaf and won't miss the bread at all, unless that is, you've made up the Keto bread recipe you discovered in this book! You can still enjoy your favorite pasta dishes, even taco salad, but without the grogginess in the afternoon that comes with all those unnecessary carbs.

So, energize your life and sustain a healthy body by applying what you've discovered. You don't have to change everything at once. Just start by adopting a new recipe each week that sounds interesting to you. Gradually, swap out less-than-healthy options for ingredients and recipes from this book that will promote your well-being.

Each time you make a healthy substitution or try a new ketogenic recipe, you can feel proud of yourself; you are actually taking good care of your mind and body. Even before you start to experience the benefits of a ketogenic lifestyle, you can feel good because you are choosing the best course for your life.

Thanks for reading.

Printed in Great Britain
by Amazon